Violence and Religion

Violence and Religion examines a recurring theme in history, that of the tension between religious faith and political and militant action. Judy Sproxton offers a detailed and fascinating reading of the writings of some of the major figures of the time including Calvin, d'Aubigné, Cromwell, Winstanley and the poet Andrew Marvell. Looking at texts written during two periods of major political upheaval and civil unrest in the sixteenth and seventeenth centuries, she explores the division between their different understanding of the self-interest of humanity and the will of God.

'Judy Sproxton is unusual in having a deep knowledge both of the French civil wars of the 16th century and of the 17th century English Revolution. Even more unusually, she is soaked in the literature of the two countries. In consequence her work sheds much new light on both.'

Christopher Hill

Judy Sproxton is Lecturer in French at the University of Birmingham.

Violence and Religion

Attitudes towards militancy in the
French civil wars and the English
Revolution

Judy Sproxton

London and New York

For Nick

First published 1995
by Routledge
11 New Fetter Lane, London EC4P 4EE

Simultaneously published in the USA and Canada
by Routledge
29 West 35th Street, New York, NY 10001

© 1995 Judy Sproxton

Typeset in Palatino by Michael Mepham, Frome, Somerset
Printed and bound in Great Britain by
Mackays of Chatham PLC, Chatham, Kent

British Library Cataloguing in Publication Data
A catalogue record for this book is available from
the British Library

Library of Congress Cataloging in Publication Data
Sproxton, Judy.
 Violence and religion: attitudes towards militancy
 in the French civil wars and the English Revolution /
 Judy Sproxton.
 p. cm.
 Includes bibliographical references and index.
 ISBN 0-415-07681-1: $49.00 (U.S.)
 1. Militarism—Religious aspects—Christianity—
 History of doctrines. 2. Calvin, Jean, 1509–1564.
 3. France—History—16th century. 4. Great Britain—
 History—Civil War, 1642–1649. 5. Sociology,
 Christian (Reformed) — Europe — History. I. Title.
 BT736.2.S63 1994   94-25049
                                                          CIP

ISBN 0–415–07681–1

Contents

Acknowledgements

I should like to thank many people for their encouragement, stimulus and help. Christopher Hill has kindly shown an interest in my work since I first started to see parallels in the thought of French writers in the civil wars and English writers of the time of the Revolution. Terence Cave helped me to understand political writing in the context of devotional literature. Thanks are due to friends and colleagues of the University of Birmingham for their knowledge and advice, including Tony Davies, Robert Wilcher, Nigel Wood and, latterly, Nicholas Hammond.

I am grateful to the editor of the *Journal of European Studies* for giving me permission to reproduce a substantial amount of 'Perspectives of war in the writing of Agrippa d'Aubigné', which originally appeared in the journal.

Above all, I want to thank my husband, Nick, who has joined me in wrestling with these ideas.

Judy Sproxton,
Temple Grafton,
February 1994

Abbreviations

The following abbreviations have been used in this text:

I.C.   Jean Calvin (1957–68) *Institution de la Religion Chrestienne,* Paris, ed. J. Benoit: 5 vols.

L.T.   Agrippa d'Aubigné (1962–7) *Les Tragiques,* Paris, ed. A. Garnier and J. Plattard.

Abbott   W.C. Abbott, ed., (1937–47) *The Letters and Speeches of Oliver Cromwell,* Cambridge, Mass.: 4 vols.

Introduction

> If there is anything in mortal affairs which should be approached with hesitancy, or rather which ought to be avoided in every possible way, guarded against and shunned, that thing is war; there is nothing more wicked, more disastrous, more widely destructive, more deeply tenacious, more loathsome, in a word, more unworthy of man, not to say of a Christian.
>
> (Phillips 1967: 107)

So wrote Erasmus in the 1515 edition of his *Adages*. In bringing to bear on the climate of his times his great Humanist scholarship together with his evangelical faith, Erasmus was among the first to challenge the prevalent attitudes and activities of church and state.

Within a few years, any such criticism was to arouse suspicion and hostility. Before long, violence was considered by many authorities throughout Europe as the only means to suppress challenge. Many of those who questioned the integrity of their rulers equally had recourse to the sword in an effort to protect freedom of worship.

The aim of this book, however, is not to assess the political consequences of Reform movements in the sixteenth century. I have chosen rather to look more specifically at the effect the new climate of challenge had on certain individuals. The priority given by the Reform to the will of God over human institutions led to an invigorating freedom to define personal moral stance.

The writers I have chosen to discuss in the following pages have in common their readiness to identify, in one way or another, the working of the will of God in the context of a climate of social upheaval.

The men to whose writings I refer came from vastly different social backgrounds. John Calvin was an exegete and a preacher; he encountered his fellow citizens from the pulpit. Agrippa d'Aubigné was an aristocrat, a soldier and a poet. The Monomachs were all but anonymous pamphleteers, seeking deliberately to stir social unrest. Oliver Cromwell came from a small landowning family in Cambridgeshire. Gerrard Winstanley's father was a cloth merchant; he himself became a cow herdsman. Andrew Marvell was a tutor, then a diplomat in Milton's ministry of Foreign Tongues, and later an MP for Hull in the opposition after the Restoration.

The texts left by these men indicate their personal understanding of the relation between the will of God and the resources of man. They also express the degree of confidence they had in the action they thought most appropriate to God's will. This, of course, includes their views on the appropriateness of armed conflict.

From an historical point of view, the French civil wars and the English Revolution have little in common. The French civil wars of the late sixteenth century were concerned with a struggle for power between aristocrats. The English Revolution was politically more substantial, introducing the organized power of a new force. The success of Cromwell's New Model Army led to a basic constitutional upheaval, which had considerable effect on men's lives throughout England and also on the way in which they understood their role in society. It would be impossible to find many parallels between these historical moments. On the other hand, the thought proceeding from the Reform movement on the continent and subsequently in England in the sixteenth century contributed substantially to the way in which these social upheavals were understood. It is the spiritual interpretation offered by the writers I discuss which, to me, make comparison of them so interesting: each of them was endeavouring to persuade his readers or listeners of the metaphysical significance of social struggle.

I hope that close textual consideration of the writings of the authors I have selected leads to a reconstruction of the terms of their understanding. Although I hope to have included sufficient introductory references to put these writers in the perspective of the times in which they wrote, I have no wish to present my observations as an historical study. My aim is to express their views in their own terms, and to suggest how they themselves interpreted their own situation. Each of them sought to express the challenge of his time in a way that would create a vivid response in the minds of his contemporaries and would clarify his ideas in his own mind.

All of them thought to be writing *sub specie aeternitatis*, but this very perspective was established differently in the mind of each.

I have chosen to discuss these particular writers because of the differences in the way they wrote, in the way they identified the challenge of the social situation in which they lived, and in the way they understood the relationship between man and God. I have not sought at any point to establish links between them, nor to impose a theoretical evaluation of the ideas they embraced into which each might neatly fit. What I wish to emphasize is how each writer draws on different sources and seeks for a different impact.

For all these differences, I have found Calvin's categoric qualification of human resources to be an ever-present concept in all these writers' thinking, although it is used in different ways – sometimes to diminish the extravagant claims of others, sometimes to diminish the confidence of the writer himself. My intention when I began this study was to separate the writers on whom I had chosen to focus: however, when I had pursued my reading further, I realized that, although there is no consistent line of thought that runs through the work of them all, Calvin's robust challenge of human adequacy has a part to play throughout.

Chapter 1

Calvin: violent remedies

REPRESSION OF WILL

Calvin was considerably behind Luther in introducing into his pronouncements any concept of active resistance. Although he is often seen as a decisive influence on armed uprising, there is virtually no evidence in his writing that he condoned such actions. The fact that his followers did eventually resort to arms can be attributed far less to Calvin's writings and sermons than to the pressure of circumstance, since they were harrassed to the point of seeing peril for the Church in acquiescence. Although it is important to consider Calvin's involvement in the Conspiration d'Amboise, which marked the point of overt intervention on the part of the Reformers in affairs of state, it is in many ways more important to examine the moral directive offered by Calvin to his followers in the *Institution Chrestienne*, which appeared in French translation in Geneva in 1541. It is here that we find expressed the disparity between the life of the spirit and activity in society which comprised much of the substance of Calvin's teaching and established a perspective which, for some, endured.

The separation between worldly concerns and the spiritual priorities of the faithful Christian was a fundamental theme in the *Institution Chrestienne*. Many of Calvin's pamphlets insisted on the importance of an uncompromising public stance (Calvin 1970) and indeed deplored as idolatry any ambiguity in the conduct of a man who appeared to condone forms of worship which his conscience did not endorse. However, the principal theme of the *Institution Chrestienne* is the transcendance of man's everyday, secular identity: the goal of all men must be moral regeneration, and consciousness of the spiritual dimension of existence must ultimately render them indifferent to the transactions of the material world. To make this point, Calvin paraphrases St Paul:

> Ceux qui usent de ce monde y doyvent avoir aussi peu d'affection comme s'ils n'en usoyent point.

> Those who are involved in this world should be as little attached to it as if they were not.

(I.C.: III.X.4)

None the less, while asserting the primacy of matters of faith and the importance of the interior response to the word of God, Calvin was wary not to go to the other extreme and claim with the Anabaptists that social laws and military duties were to be excluded altogether from the life of the Christian. He recognized the value of the secular organization of the community, not for its own sake, but inasmuch as it might provide a channel for the dedication of the individual to the will of God. It was unrealistic, he claimed, to attempt to ignore the organization of society altogether; man's nature was such that he could not pretend that social concerns had no place in his life:

> Si la volonté du Seigneur est telle, que nous cheminions sur terre à nostre vray pays, davantage si telles aydes sont necessaires à nostre voyage, ceux que les veulent séparer de l'homme luy ostent sa nature humaine.

> If such is the will of the Lord that we should travel on earth towards our real country, and all the more if these experiences are necessary to our spiritual journey, those who wish to separate them from man take from him his human nature.

(I.C.: IV.XX.2)

Such importance as social considerations might have, then, pertained manifestly to 'la nature humaine'. They might in some way constitute a beneficial challenge to the persistence of the individual, but were, in themselves, far removed from the order of the things of God. Calvin classed them amongst the 'choses terriennes', those temporal matters which were but details encountered in the course of the great spiritual journey and were, as St Augustine had said, overrated by the ungodly (St Augustine 1924: Vol. I, 312) The 'choses terriennes' were practical, human matters which might easily be controlled and understood with a little common sense:

Nul n'est destitué de la lumière de la raison quant au gouverne-
ment de la vie presenté.

No one is deprived of the light of reason in matters of the
organization of immediate life.

(I.C.: II.II.13)

Calvin is often cited as the practical force behind the Reformation
and even as an innovator of certain lines of political organization.
But although his theology promoted an active, social expression of
religious commitment, he subscribed to the Stoic view that there
was no inherent value in particular forms of conduct:

Quant est des actions, lesquelles de soy ne sont ni bonnes ni
mauvaises, et appartiennent plustost à la vie terrienne que spirituelle . . .

As far as actions are concerned, which in themselves are neither
good nor bad, and belong to earthly rather than spiritual life . . .

(I.C.: II.IV.6)

All actions, unless they implied a spiritual directive or aim, were
in themselves insignificant and circumscribed by human limitations. Further restrictions on action did not hamper the spiritual
pilgrimage:

La liberté spirituelle peut très bien consister avec la servitude
civile.

Spiritual freedom is certainly able to exist alongside civil servitude.

(I.C.: II.II.13)

The only achievement possible for man, according to Calvin's
theology, was an acknowledgement of his own impotence and of
God's greatness. He must accept the necessity of the intrusion of
social demands as a reminder of his inadequacies, rather than see
in them a worthwhile pursuit.

The consequence of Calvin's theology was a counsel of patience
in the face of affliction. To rebel against the social order and to
attempt to reorganize it implied a false confidence in man's ability
to improve on the will of God: the social order, however unjust it
might appear, was allowed by God and as such should be re-
spected. It is ironic in a sense that Calvin should have been called
upon to advise the government of Geneva, a responsibility he is

known to have resented. This role has given him a reputation for a concern with political organization which does not reflect his priorities, and which distorts the view expressed in the *Institution Chrestienne* that such organization had no intrinsic worth. In fact, the only importance accorded by Calvin to involvement in social issues was that they might offer the faithful Christian an opportunity to assert the value of self effacement and praise of God. Indeed, such values might be more effectively upheld, and with greater benefit to the individual, if the social structure itself denied them. It was not Calvin's view that Christian values could be expressed by attempts to organize a society based on brotherly love, as Erasmus had perhaps envisaged. To Calvin, the inconsistencies and imperfections to be found in human affairs, far from constituting a deviation from man's nature, in fact characterized it. They were indications of the distance between God's perfection and the inadequacy of human resources. The Fall had meant that man could never govern himself with the enlightenment with which God had originally endowed him; all subsequent failure was directly attributable to original sin:

> L'Homme estant en sa nature antique n'a rien en qui ne fust honnorable. Dont il s'ensuit que tout ce qui nous est à honte et opprobre, doit estre imputé à nostre faute.

> In his original state, there was nothing dishonourable in Man. Therefore, it follows that everything shameful and unworthy in us, must be blamed on our own fault.

> (Calvin 1554: 41)

If there were inequalities in society, this was a necessary consequence of man's original disobedience. His first rebellion had distanced him irrevocably from ideal harmony. Further rebellion would distance him yet more, as it would imply a misplaced trust in his own resources to put things right. In the absence of a capacity to act as a perpetrator of divine values, man must follow the dictates of necessity, coping as best he might and resisting his illusions of knowing better. His conduct in society must reflect his acknowledgement of the imperfection of all human institutions. Of course, it was to be hoped that secular rulers would follow the moral guidance of the Scriptures. But the best means to ensure that the consciences of such leaders be enlightened was through prayer. God was to lead, man to follow. The faithful Christian distinguished himself from his ungodly fellows not by showing that he was better able to organize society but by his awareness of its essential imperfection.

Mesnard defined Calvin's political attitude as:

> Ni un conformisme enthousiaste, ni un scepticisme absolu, mais un sain loyalisme.

> Neither an enthusiastic desire to conform, nor an absolute scepticism, but a sober loyalty.

> (Mesnard 1956: 289)

This loyalty, however, did not of course imply an unqualified recognition of secular power, for acquiescence to the authority of a prince did not constitute an endorsement of that prince's policies. It was more a token of submission to God's will, however arduous the consequences, and a curbing of worldly ambition. It was a greater achievement from Calvin's point of view to tolerate iniquities than to contest them, especially if that tolerance contributed to maintain good order in society. Necessity, in such cases, demanded an overt co-operation, although it did not demand an identification with the policy behind the obligation imposed:

> Toutes loix humaines . . . ne lient point la conscience, pource que la necessité de les observer ne gist point aux choses qu'elles commandent, comme si c'estoit peché de soy, faire cecy ou cela; mais que le tout se doit rapporter à la fin générale, c'est qu'il y ait bon ordre et police entre nous.

> No human law binds the conscience, because the importance of observing these does not lie in what they command, as if they in themselves defined sin, but that obeying them leads to good order and organization amongst us.

> (I.C.: IV.X.5)

The very division established by Calvin between acquiescence before the social order and acceptance of its values contained an implicit challenge which inevitably had political consequences. Whilst emphasizing the necessity of conserving good order in society, Luther and Calvin would not subscribe to the mystique which traditionally surrounded the monarch, and felt justified in using very plain language in their dealings with princes. The tone of Calvin's dediction of the *Institution Chrestienne* to Francis I held an undeniable note of challenge:

Le Seigneur Roy des Rois veuille establir vostre Throne en justice
et vostre siege en equité, très fort et très illustre Roy.

May the Lord who is king of kings establish your throne in
justice and your rule in equity, most strong and illustrious king.
(Epistre au Roy, I.C.: 49)

Such condescension could not be confused with flattery. Calvin
clearly considered that the guidance of the Reformed Church alone
could provide the king with the moral authority to justify his rule,
and that, however many 'absolute rights' his lawyers drew up for
Francis, these could be no substitute for the basic precepts of
Biblical authority. The Christian fidelity postulated in the *Institution Chrestienne* denied authority to all but God, and therefore the
concept of right rule could only have meaning in terms of the
values defined in the Scriptures. Mystique and human tradition, in
Calvin's view, could only obscure these values and were to be
condemned. Reformers following Calvin's observations were in no
doubt that they owed allegiance primarily to the precepts of the
Scriptures and that the person of the monarch possessed no inherent authority. However, since these precepts included respect for
the order which God's will had permitted and sustained, there was
no explicit nor even implicit tendency to sedition in this stance.

Overtly, the faithful Christian was to accept the social order in
which he found himself. On an inner level, it was essential that he
be able to transcend the distractions of the 'choses terriennes' and
concern himself with the realities of the human condition. The
distinction Calvin made between the earthly and the celestial orders was intended as a warning against man's tendency to become
involved in immediate issues at the expense of more fundamental
concerns, and to delude himself that he could find in a secular
context what could only be sought in the divine. Scope for rejection
of sin and espousal of God's will were his basic needs, and these
could be found in terms of his battle with himself rather than in
debates on the organization of society. A concern with the righting
of social wrongs was, in Calvin's view, the result of the seduction
of reason. On one level, it would appear rational to man to intervene with the aim of promoting justice in the social order; on
another level, from the perspective which reduced human concepts
of justice to insignificance, such an act would be reprehensible:

non seulement le commun, mais les philosophes, réputent que

c'est l'acte le plus noble et excellent qu'on saurait faire que de déliverer son pais de tyrannie. Au contraire, tout homme privé qui aura violé un tirant est apertement condamné par la voix de Dieu.

not only the common man, but philosophers, claim that it is the noblest and most excellent act possible to deliver one's country from tyranny. On the contrary, any private citizen who assaults a tyrant is clearly condemned by the voice of God.

(I.C.: III.X.6)

Calvin's appeal to his fellow Christians was for a moral regeneration which alone could help to arrest the tide of evil which he saw engulfing mankind. Although Calvin commended a relative indifference towards the organization of secular affairs, he urged all faithful Christians to be on the alert for the presence of evil and to combat it strenuously with penitence and prayer. His introduction to the *Institution Chrestienne* creates an image of mankind on the threshold of total disaster which only extreme remedies might allay:

Ceux qui ne sont du tout aveugles appercoivent que quasi plusiers mers de maux sont desbordées sur la terre, et que tout le monde est corrompu de plusieurs pestes mortelles, brief que tout tombe en ruine tellement qu'il faut ou du tout désesperer des choses humaines ou mettre ordre à tels maux par remedes violens.

Those who are not completely blind perceive that many seas of sin are flooding the earth, and that the whole world is corrupted by mortal plagues; in short, that all things are falling apart to such a point that, either all aspects of human life are to be despaired of, or such evils must be amended by violent remedies.

(Epistre au Roy, I.C.: 40)

The 'remedes violens' of which Calvin speaks are, of course, nothing to do with bloodshed. They involve a remorseless attack of man on himself, condemning his blindness and folly, rejecting his enslavement to sin and admitting that he is totally indebted to God and without resources to save himself. The afflictions which beset man have resulted from his compliance with the forces of sin. Only grace can save him, and he must acknowledge his need of it.

Calvin's appraisal of man's relation with God in the *Institution Chrestienne* was itself part of what he saw as extreme action; he felt a responsibility to impart to his fellows what he had been allowed to see so clearly and to warn them that they disregarded these insights at their peril.

Although Calvin's advice made it clear that the inner struggle with sin took priority over all other concerns, the establishment of a government in Geneva under the auspices of the Reformed Church made it necessary to define ways in which Christian fidelity might be expressed communally in a social context. The *Institution Chrestienne*, for the benefit of those Christians who lived under an unenlightend rule, points out that the challenge offered in such a situation to the Christian is to resist his desire to correct apparent injustice and to concentrate instead on penitence and prayer. For the Christians living in Geneva, however, obedience to laws framed in acknowledgment of God's supremacy involved more than an overt submission. Such obedience meant more than an effort to maintain order; it was a channel for the positive expression of faith. In his treatise of 1560, *De L'Authorité des Magistrats en la Punition des Heretiques,* de Bèze endeavoured to establish the aspects of social responsibility which were identifiable as spiritual obligations. At the point where protection of the integrity of the Church is at stake, de Bèze writes, civil and divine considerations merge:

> tant le Droict civil que le Droict coustumier est en partie Divin, c'est à dire, concernant le service de Dieu, et la conscience, en partie appertenant aux affaires humaines, et à la vie externe.

> civil law as much as common law is in part divine, that is to say, it concerns the service of God and the conscience, both belonging in part to human affairs and external activity.

(de Bèze 1560: 37)

A vital distinction is established in this tract separating those social matters which were mere questions of organization and material possessions, and those which had spiritual significance and must be referred to the conscience before God. De Bèze states that there are aspects of conduct which relate to the divine and that these are distinguishable by the complete absence of self-interest in the hearts of those who pursue them. When assertion of the will of God is the only concern, public acts become spiritually meaningful.

Again, de Bèze follows the Augustinian division between the things of man and the things of God, but he is careful not to distinguish between the private and the public man; in a society where man is exhorted to fulfil his Christianity in the community, they are on a par. The act which pursues self-advancement is of no worth; it is relegated to the city of man, which

> cherche seulement ses commoditez, et s'appuye sur sa prudence. Quant a Dieu, ou elle le mesprise du tout, ou le concevant selon la fausse imagination de son entendement le sert d'un service inventé à sa poste: et ce ou du tout par feintise . . . Au contraire, l'autre cité est tout addonnée à son Createur, tellement qu'elle ne se donne point congé de rien faire que par la bouche et la comandement d'iceluy, et rapporte à l' avancement de la gloire et louange de cestuy la, tout ce qu'elle fait en public et en particulier.

> looks only to its own interests and relies on its own prudence. As for God, either [the city of man] rejects him altogether, or, conceiving him according to its own whim, serves him according to its own fantasy or through mere pretence . . . On the other hand, the [city of God] is totally committed to its Creator, to such an extent that it allows itself no action but in obedience to his commandment, and refers to the promotion of his glory and praise, all that it does both in public and private.
>
> (de Bèze 1560: 35)

This treatise was designed to underline the responsibility of a magistrate to curb heresy; such was his moral duty before God, and was in the spiritual interests of the community. In this way, de Bèze defined the moral good of the community as a spur to action, as long as this action was not tainted with self-interest.

To the extent that secular power was already in the hands of the magistrates in Geneva, it was legitimate that Calvin and subsequently de Bèze should advise them on how best to use it in the light of spiritual priorities. The harmony, or rather unison, of the spiritual and the secular was a clearly desirable aim.

However, the views of Calvin and de Bèze on the nature of public acts on the part of Christians living in an unenlightened society had a degree of ambiguity. Calvin had stated that no compromise was possible in matters which related to proper worship of God. Yet he also stressed the importance of acquiescing before the rule of the secular monarch, however tyrannical. As Reformers became increasingly persecuted in France and elsewhere, the quandary arose as to how these attacks should be met. De Bèze's treatise quoted above is concerned with the authority of magistrates in a Christian community, yet it asserts as a premise the importance of setting the moral welfare of the community above other considerations. Inevitably, Reformers whose freedom of worship was curbed regarded such infringement as a direct assault on the consciences of the community; this was not mere tyranny over body or possessions.

Calvin throughout his life insisted on the primacy of repentance and the power of prayer. On hearing the news of attacks on members of the Reformed faith in Germany in 1545, he delivered a sermon in Geneva deploring the attacks but warning that the fate of individuals was unimportant; what mattered was the peril to the Church. It could not be said that individuals did not deserve tribulation; the wrong of the attacks lay in their manifest opposition to the will of God, and as such they must be resisted:

> Quand nous pensons à nous: il n'y à qu'occasion d'estre troublez mais quand nous regardons ceux qui nous font la guerre non point pour nos vices, combien à que tu nous pouvois punir pour iceux, mais qu'ils veulent ruiner le Regne de ton filz, qui doit estre maintenu par toy, c'est le fondement de nostre hardiesse.

> When we think of ourselves: we have only to think of our unworthiness, but when we see those who make war on us not for our sins, however much we deserve to be punished for these, but because they wish to destroy the reign of your son which you must maintain, this provides the source of our resistance.
>
> (Calvin 1546: non pag.)

The 'hardiesse' of which Calvin speaks is fundamentally a moral resistance. The Reformers, he claimed, would not make the mistake of believing that resistance to the enemies of the Church was a matter of material strength:

> Les iniques, les infideles se confieront en leurs chariotz et chevaux, en leurs lances et espees, mais nous esperons au nom du Seigneur notre Dieu.

> The wicked, the infidels will trust in their horses and chariots,

in their lances and swords, but we will hope in the name of the
Lord our God.

(Calvin 1546: non pag.)

As individuals, Calvin emphasized, Christians must consider all
affliction as a reminder of their personal unworthiness. But as
aspiring agents of the will of God, they must be prepared to put
behind them all thought of physical safety. Their confidence in the
will of God must be so great as to make them discount such
considerations as material loss; to assume that circumstantial evidence suggested indications of God's favour or the lack of it was
greatly to underestimate the power of grace. The enemies of the
Reformed Church, Calvin declared, would be only too ready to do
just this, as they put their faith in works and claimed merit for their
own actions. Calvin urged prayer and penitence as the weapons
wherewith to counter attacks on the Reformers, maintaining that
the faithful Christian could never be defeated if he placed all his
faith in God's will and his moral energy into accepting its course.

REPRESSION OF ARMED HOSTILITY

The involvement of the Reformers in militant activity is difficult to
reconcile with their insistence on a religion free from worldly
concerns and was indeed something of a paradox in terms of their
own thought. Luther's opposition to the corruption of the papacy
and the iniquities of the administration within the Roman Catholic
Church did not imply an assertion of any human capacity to
remedy injustice; he was anxious above all to separate political
opportunism from matters of faith and to expose the Roman
Church as using its claim to spiritual power merely as a means of
advancing its secular interests. Luther's political following embar-
rassed him as is well known. His denunciation of corruption was
not intended as a signal to the peasants to claim their rights.
However, in his book *The Foundations of Modern Political Thought*,
Quentin Skinner points out how Luther had established in the
1530s an argument that a secular authority only possessed that
authority in so far as he performed his duties responsibly (Skinner
1978: II, 202). When Luther was asked in 1539 if it would be
legitimate to resist the emperor on behalf of the Gospel, he replied
that it was justifiable to kill in self-defence, an argument drawn
from civil law. The implication of Luther's reply, as Skinner points

out, is that the ruler ceases to be God's delegate once he departs from the proper dispensation of his duties and may be regarded as a private individual. This point of view was developed by Bucer in his later edition of the *Explications of the Four Gospels* and the posthumously published *Commentaries on the Book of Judges* (1554) (see Skinner 1978: II, 207), where he declares that when the ruler fails to uphold God's ordinance, the inferior magistrates are obliged to resist his rule and that ultimately they must attempt to remove him by force of arms.

Calvin's efforts were directed towards emphasizing the moral challenge of a situation in which Reformers were attacked, seeing in it an opportunity to exercise the discipline of patience and prayer. There can be no doubt that the propagation of the Reformed faith was very well organized from Geneva. It has been established that the training and dispatch of pastors from Geneva to France from the beginning of the 1560s resulted in a network of Protestant centres throughout the country (Kingdon 1956). These missionaries were not an overt political threat and Catherine de Medici had agreed that they might be sent, although the routes they took were deliberately left undefined. There is no evidence to suggest that the missionaries had any aim other than the evangelizing of the people. They did not concern themselves with the balance of power between Bourbon and Guise at court. Robert Kingdon suggests that it was likely, although there is no proof, that some of these pastors did in fact become leaders of resistance in their own areas; some were persecuted and even executed for suspected involvement (it is notable that they were accused of sedition rather than heresy, since the policy of appeasement briefly attempted by Catherine had established a distinction between the two). However, Kingdon's researches suggest that these men were, on the whole, trying to quell insurrection rather than to incite it. Their mission was to evangelize, even if the excellent organization behind this enterprise lent itself well to political ends. It would, however, be unjustifiable to assume that it was framed with such intentions.

There can be no doubt that the conspiracy of Amboise of 1560 marked a point at which political and religious considerations merged to the point of being virtually indistinguishable. The death of Henri II, whose antagonism towards the Protestants had been consistently savage, created a vacuum in the power structure which tempted many Protestants to envisage the possibility of the establishment of a ruler who might prove more sympathetic towards them. Although they had been patient throughout Henri's aggression, following Calvin's counsel not to attack the Lord's anointed, they could not help but look to the opportunity of increasing freedom of worship which could be offered under the rule of another authority; naturally, their hopes lay in the king of Navarre. François de Morel, the new Protestant leader, tried to persuade Navarre into action, and, from his correspondence with Calvin, it can be deduced that the latter was keen that the Protestants might take advantage of Navarre's rank as prince of the Royal blood.

Although Morel received specific instructions from Calvin, these are not available and evidence of Calvin's position can be found in Morel's reply alone (Sutherland 1967: 16). It was clear, however, that Calvin wished Navarre to take up an authoritative position in court and embark on a policy which might be favourable to the Protestants. It appears that Calvin's interest was more than merely theoretical and that he had a predetermined plan for placing Navarre in power, although it is not clear what this plan was. Calvin's instructions appear to have called for a *coup d'état* with the help of foreign aid. It is also clear that Calvin did envisage the use of force in this attempt, despite his consistent preaching of patience and obedience.

The reason why Calvin committed himself politically on this occasion, whilst rejecting totally the idea of rebellion against the power that God had established on earth, was that Navarre did have legitimate claim to govern, and that to install him in power would not entail any infringement of what was legally valid. In response to pressure from Calvin, Morel did what he could to encourage Navarre to take some assertive course of action, and to reduce his fears. In his report to Calvin, Morel states how he tried to reassure Navarre that his attempts to dislodge the Guises from their position of influence would meet with considerable support. Navarre assumed that Calvin was relying on the German princes, and doubted their dependability himself. Navarre was not prepared at this stage to take up the proposition presented to him on Calvin's behalf by Morel. Morel asked of Calvin whether there were any other possibilities of coming to the aid of the Church, since he had doubts about Navarre's readiness to assert his rights.

Calvin, of course, had constantly emphasized that prayer was the only reliable resource, yet Morel felt compelled to enquire whether there might not be any 'moyens moins sublimes'. He pointed out that when a minor ascended to the throne, the Estates General should be summoned to appoint tutors and counsellors and that possibly anyone had the right to insist on this, using armed force if necessary.

The betrayal of the Protestant meeting places in Paris led to the discovery of incriminating papers suggesting that there were plots against the Guises amongst them, and the actual conspiracy of Amboise probably resulted from several different stages of deliberation. Jurists and theologians of France and Germany were approached to establish the legality of armed uprising against the illegal usurpation of government by the Guises, and the Prince of Conde was approached to give his sanction to such an act as prince of the Royal blood. La Renaudie offered his services, although he did not have Calvin's approval. It is a matter of speculation how far Protestant ministers were involved in the plotting at this point. It is possible that La Roche de Chandieu, a principal minister, approached Condé. It is impossible, however, to find evidence for the ministers' full involvement in the plot, although they and Calvin undeniably supported the notion of legitimate opposition to the Guises (Sutherland 1967: 19).

When Calvin, de Bèze and Chandieu were accused in 1561 of complicity in the conspiracy, Chandieu denied having reported to the French Churches that the Genevan ministry endorsed the enterprise. Chandieu stated that Calvin had regarded the state of affairs as a purely civil matter and had said that there was no harm in restoring proper order to France if this were done without effusion of blood. One cannot tell from this, however, to what degree Calvin was prepared to support the use of armed force. In Calvin's letter to Coligny of 16 April 1561, his suspicions of the outcome of plans for resistance are very clear. He has no objection to the princes of the Royal blood and the parliament asserting their rights in the name of the common good, but he was fearful of the consequences of any bloodshed. It appears that Chandieu was readier than Calvin to accept Condé as the necessary prince of the blood to embark on the enterprise of dislodging the Guises. The meeting organized by La Renaudie in Nantes on 1 February 1560 was concerned with emphasizing the impropriety of the Guises. He asked the members of the meeting to support an attempt to seize the Guises, to assemble the Estates General and provide the young king with suitable guidance. Support was agreed to, and the date for the act was fixed for 10 March. La Renaudie went to Paris to see Conde and to raise men, arms and horses.

When the conspiracy was betrayed, La Renaudie was killed. Documents were taken from his secretary, La Bigne, which stated the position of the Protestant involvement in the affair. They claimed that, as far as their religious commitment was concerned, this was a separate matter from the question of service to the king. They disclaimed all support for sedition and reasserted their principle of obedience. The Guises were not impressed by this claim.

It is clear the Protestant involvement in the whole affair was initiated by the intolerable position in which they had found themselves towards the end of the 1550s. It was the last time that Calvin had himself contemplated political means to assist the Church, and it was only the possibility of a bloodless *coup* that led him to this consideration. There was, in his eyes, no subsequent legitimate alternative. The attitudes which emerged after the massacre of Vassy were not consistent with Calvin's continued deprecation of bloodshed. Basically, his view cannot be said to have changed (Geisendorf 1949: 179–80).

It is largely a matter of opinion how the Reformers themselves changed in their attitude to the legitimacy of armed resistance, since the more militant became increasingly the more articulate. Certainly their initial patience inspired respect even from those who disagreed with them, and Ronsard himself (retrospectively) admired them. However, the conviction that Calvin and de Bèze had been involved directly in the Conspiracy of Amboise rapidly spread.

There is also evidence to suggest that Reformers were protecting themselves with arms; one of the terms of the 1562 *Edit de Janvier* was that the Reformers should not wear arms at services. However, after the massacre of Vassy at the beginning of March, Reformers began increasingly to disregard this injunction; de Bèze delivered a sermon where he was protected by Conde's forces. De Bèze was in fact often chided in contemporary pamphlets for arming himself, although he was reputed to have justified himself by saying, 'les armes entre les mains des sages portent la paix' ('arms in the hands of the wise bring peace'). Calvin, on the other hand, even after the massacre of Vassy, deprecated the notion of a minister carrying arms:

Ce n'est pas un acte décent qu'un ministre se face soudart ou capitaine: mais c'est beaucoup pis quand on quitte la chaire pour porter les armes.

It is improper that a minister should become a soldier or a captain but it is much worse when he descends from his pulpit to take up arms.

(Calvin 1854: II, 466)

Pamphleteers, including Ronsard, writing against the Reformers did their best to credit them with embarking on a policy of armed aggression, which, they objected, was a contradiction to their profession of following Christ. The notion that they preached an 'Evangile armée' did much to alienate the popular view of Reformers and to increase hostility towards them as being responsible for the state of war; de Bèze had no compunction in asserting the legal right of Reformers to defend themselves. In doing so, he claimed, they were only endeavouring to uphold the Royal statute, since the *Edit de Janvier* had forbidden persecution of the Reformers. De Bèze wrote to the Duc de Nevers:

Voila donc pour le jourduy la disposition de nos affaires laquelle nous contrainct de nostre coste de regarder s'il y a quelque juste moyen, non point d'offenser noz ennemis, pour lesquels plustost nous prions tous les jours et de coeur et de bouche, en rendant le bien pour le mal comme il nous est commandé de nostre Dieu, mais pour nous garder à ce qu'un tel outrage ne nous soit faict contre les deffenses expresses du Roy.

That is how the state of affairs stands at the moment, which is compelling us to consider if there might be any just way, certainly not of harming our enemies, for whom we would rather pray night and day with heart and voice, returning good for evil as God commanded, but to protect ourselves from outrageous attack which might be committed against us against the specific orders of the king.

(de Bèze 1960–83: IV, 71)

He continues:

Nous ne pouvons juger qu'il ne nous soit licite, par tout droict divin et humain, et sans contrevenir à la volonté du roy, avoir recours à ceux qui peuvent contre garder nostre innocence par leur authorité, conseil et puissance.

We cannot tell if it be lawful, by all divine and human right, and
without contravening the will of the king, to call on those who
are in a position to protect our innocence through their authority, counsel and power.

(de Bèze (1960–83: LV, 71)

It is clear here that, far from seeing resistance to persecution as a
step against established secular authority, de Bèze is presenting the
position of the Reformers as an active endorsement of Royal policy.
On the other hand, de Bèze does not appear to have been as
reluctant as Calvin to accept that armed resistance was a legitimate
means of securing their welfare. De Bèze considered arms necessary if the freedom of worship of the Reformers were to be
protected; the disruption of the service at Vassy was an outrage
which offered the Reformers a spiritual challenge: they must defend their right to do God's will. Although Montaigne was
probably right in his observation that many of the instigators of the
war fought only 'sous prétexte de religion', there was a strong
movement amongst the ecclesiastical leaders at this time to assert
as boldly as possible the rights of the Reformers to freedom of
worship, and to insist that these rights be protected by arms. De
Bèze, Badius and other ecclesiastical leaders all resisted the em-
ployment of manoeuvre and strategy to obtain any settlement
which might infringe these rights merely for the sake of peace.

The recourse to arms in 1562 was a turning point in the history
of the Reformers' response to persecution, but the massacre of St
Bartholomew's Day ten years later was decisive in establishing in
the minds of the Reformers that the monarchy of Charles IX was a
tyrannical power.

Chapter 2

Perspectives of war in the writings of Agrippa d'Aubigné

After the massacre of St Bartholomew's Day in 1572, many writers who identified with the Reformers justified armed resistance. Agrippa d'Aubigné began to write in this period, and continued throughout his long life to present the events of his time in terms of his faith. However, d'Aubigné saw man's relationship with God as the focal point of life. In various genres, d'Aubigné wrote to acknowledge his acquiescence before the will of God, and his rejection of human self-interest. D'Aubigné did not write theology, but endeavoured to express the action of the will of God in terms of human experience. The events he witnessed in the course of his life, which lasted until the first quarter of the seventeenth century, showed him clearly the disastrous consequences of men following their own interests and ignoring the will of God. The relation between war and sin is predominant in the themes he develops.

Calvin counselled reflection on the relationship of the inner man with God, but also stressed the significance of events in the world around. Although on one level worldly matters could be seen as mere distraction, history might be acknowledged as a means used by God to make himself known to man. We find in d'Aubigné's writing a concern with both the inner and the outer man. He wished to evaluate the events of his time as an expression of God's will, but also he wished to consider his own plight as a human being in need of grace. It is possible to build up from his different writings a view of war which makes of it a focal point in the consideration of man's need of God. However, each work expresses this need in a particular way.

D'Aubigné's own ideal approach to war is perhaps best exemplified by the utter impersonality with which he speaks of it in his *Histoire Universelle*. In this extensive work, he aimed to document the period in which he lived without passing any judgement at all. In a letter to a friend written in 1616, the year of publication of the *Histoire*, he stresses the impartiality with which he described the events of St Bartholomew's Day:

> pour eschantillon de ma modestie j'ay descrit la Sainct Barthelemi sans avoir usé du mot de cruauté.

> to demonstrate my restraint, I have described the St Bartholomew massacre without once using the word 'cruelty'.

(d'Aubigné 1967: I, 475)

In Vol. I of the *Histoire* he presents the outbreak of hostilities whereby the wars began in a tone which is little more than flippant:

> apres la paix establie, les Princes, qui par elle avoyent la paix du dehors, travaillerent par emulation a qui traicteroit plus rudement ceux qu'on appelloit heretiques.
> Et de la nasquit l'ample subject de soixante ans de guerre monstrueuse que nous avons à traicter es livres suivans.

> after peace was proclaimed, the Princes, who through it had found an appearance of peace, worked one against the other to see which of them could treat more harshly those they called heretics.
> And from that point was born the ample subject of sixty years of monstrous warfare which we shall treat in the following volumes.

(d'Aubigné 1886: I, 129)

This flippancy is intended to show the genesis of the wars as human irresponsibility. Indeed, the whole narrative seeks to belittle man by implication. Sharing Calvin's view that God made himself known through history, d'Aubigné was convinced that a faithful, unadulterated account of events must inevitably reveal the judgement of God and condemn the folly of man. In the preface to the *Histoire*, d'Aubigné points out how the polarity between the nature of man and the glory of God will be easily perceived in his account:

> aisement vous tirerez de ces narrations le vrai fruict de toute l'histoire qui est de cognoistre en la folie et faiblesse des hommes le judgement et la force de Dieu.

> you will easily draw from these accounts the real lesson of all

history, which is to recognize in the folly and the weakness of men, the judgement and the strength of God.

(d'Aubigné 1886: 10)

It is interesting to see how two traditions merge in d'Aubigné's approach to history. In his close appraisal of events, he was following the Humanist criterion of authenticity, but he was also observing the division made by St Augustine in *De Civitate Dei*. In this view, the events of the temporal world have no value in themselves, but by their very imperfection they could provide a reminder of the inadequacy of humanity and its propensity to sinfulness. D'Aubigné therefore left events to speak for themselves. However, in the appendix to the work, he stresses the importance of a change of focus. The reader must turn from a consideration of the havoc of earthly things, which his history has recounted, and contemplate the celestial, where he will find permanent values. His gaze should pass

de la terre tenebreuse au ciel luisant, des splendeurs qui passent aux eternelles, des royaumes caduques au permanent, et enfin de ce qui paroist estre, vivre et regner, à ce qui seul est, vit et regne veritablement.

from the cloudy earth to the shining heaven, from splendours which fade to the eternal, from short-lived kingdoms to the everlasting and, in all, from what appears to be, to live and to reign to what alone is, lives and reigns in truth.

(d'Aubigné 1886: X, 475)

The 'ample subject' of war which constitutes the greater part of the *Histoire* stands therefore as an example of the impermanence, the delusion, the folly of human existence. Apart from pointing this out, d'Aubigné restrains himself from comment, taking the view that human terms would undermine what God has made clear in the actuality of events. There is no doubt that d'Aubigné considered his *Histoire* to be his finest work, principally because he himself is absent from it. This self-effacement reflects Calvin's theology in which the self is the source of the sin.

In d'Aubigné's political pamphlets, the folly of man is seen from a different standpoint. They express the problem of involvement in a situation which sin has engendered. Perhaps more clearly than anywhere else in his writings, d'Aubigné presents in his pamphlets the quandary of the Protestant who believed that peace of the kind demanded by God could be attained only through war. Although he asserts the necessity of armed resistance to an enemy's attacks, d'Aubigné is not belligerent in his pamphlets. He is often portrayed by modern critics as a naturally aggressive man whose fiery temperament inspired him to seek immediate vengeance for wrongs inflicted on the Protestant faction, but his pamphlets express a measured and consistent view. Emotions are checked and self-righteousness avoided in his comments on the civil disturbances and their consequences. His pamphlet *Le Caducée* appraises the divisions which had arisen amongst the Protestants after the assassination of Henri IV. It was written shortly after the Assembly of Saumur at which the Protestants were doing their best to guarantee their security while Marie de Medicis, as Regent, was trying to split their ranks.

Le Caducée points out the temptation to compromise the position of the Church and emphasizes the obligation to resist too close an alliance with the civil authorities. This pamphlet presents two opposing points of view, but does not take the form of a debate. An initial perspective is established by the narrator, who presents a criterion of Biblical wisdom against which all things are to be judged by the reader. He has the first word in the pamphlet, and reflects on the intrinsic folly of all human experience, observing how the miseries currently suffered in France are the result of indifference to the word of God:

> *Bien heureux sont ceux qui procurent la paix, car ils seront apeles Enfans de Dieu*, dit le Seigneur, & plust à Dieu que les misères des discords, soit generaux, soit particuliers, ne nous eussent point enseigné la veritté d'une tele santance, a nous qui n'ayant peu soubmettre nos pensees a l'ottorité d'un si grand Prophete, avons eu besoin du maytre des fols, qui est l'experiance.

> 'Blessed are the peacemakers, for they shall be called the children of God,' says the Lord, and would it have pleased God that the misery of discord, both general and particular, had not been necessary to teach us the truth of such a phrase, we, who, unable to submit our thoughts to the authority of so great a prophet, have had need of the master of fools, which is experience.

> (d'Aubigné 1967: II, 73)

This introduction qualifies all human experience as folly, the blind acting out of the inevitable consequences of truth established for all time in the Bible but ignored by men. Here is a similarity with the terms of d'Aubigné's *Histoire Universelle*; it is the polarity between 'la folie des hommes et la force de Dieu'. However, the lamentations of the narrator are succeeded in *Le Caducée* by an account of the different points of view of the 'prudent' and the 'ferme'. The narrator refers at the beginning to the importance of peace, but d'Aubigné shows that in the ranks of the Reformers at that time there were two ways of understanding the concept. The *prudent* thinks that obedience to the state is a means of putting an end to bloodshed:

> Nous avons consideré ces Eglises, les Ministres aux feux, les femmes & les filles violées devant les yeux des peres, & en un mot un deluge de sang par toute la France. C'est telle consideration qui nous a fait, non au plus, mais aux meilleurs, cercher la paix dans le sein de l'obeissance, & non des suretez dans celuy de la rebelion . . .

> We have considered the Churches, the Ministers burned alive, the women and young girls raped before their fathers' eyes, and, in one word, a deluge of blood throughout France. It is this consideration which has led, not all of us, but the best of us to search peace in obedience, and not surety in rebellion . . .
>
> (d'Aubigné 1967: II, 75–6)

The *prudent* goes on to say that if Marie de Medicis shows generosity towards Reformers willing to accept her authority, there is no harm in accepting it. The *ferme*, who is subsequently visited by the narrator, presents a different point of view. He claims that by nature he aspires to domestic privacy, but that he cannot accept the idea of relaxation of the military strength of the Reformers, since they have not yet won sufficient freedom to worship. It was only by a rigorous effort to maintain their physical strength that the Reformers would command the respect they needed to protect their Church. Without such strength, they would attract the contempt of their enemies, and this would lead to their continued persecution. Those who permitted the undermining of the Church's strength were responsible for the ensuing bloodshed, for only mutual fear would guarantee the avoiding of conflict.

> De ceste mutuele crainte vient la paix, lien que quiconque a voulu dissoudre, fomenter notre division, nous jetter dans le mespris, lequel & non la hayne nous fera persecuter, cettui la est

coupable devant Dieu & les hommes du vilain & sanglant estat des guerres civiles que nous avons escrit.

From this mutual fear comes peace, a link which any person who has sought to destroy, to exacerbate our differences and call contempt upon us, which is the reason for our persecution, rather than hate, that person is guilty before God and man of the wicked and bloody state of war that has been described.

(d'Aubigné 1967: II, 82–3)

The *ferme* stresses the reluctance of former Huguenot leaders to resort to armed defence. But arms, he claims, were forced on them, since their initial trust in the monarchy had been betrayed:

Vous trouverez que les brulements et massacres sans ordre de justice ont esmu les armes, les armes ont formé le Party . . .

You will find that the burnings and massacres which flouted all legal rule gave rise to the taking up of arms, and the taking up of arms formed the Party . . .

(d'Aubigné 1967: II, 86)

The only choice left to the Reformers was to resist persecution, unless they wished to die at the whim of their enemies. This tragic situation had been brought about because the civil authorities had not curbed the aggressors:

S'il y a donc quelque chose qui ne soit consonant a l'Estat que le blame en soit aux autheurs & le remede vers eux mesmes et non point vers ceux qui n'apelent point la necessité, mais la soufrent & ne contribuent pas a ce mal, si ce n'est qu'ils ne veulent pas perir au gre de leurs ennemis.

If therefore something has arisen which is beyond conformity to the state let the blame lie with the instigators and the remedy applied to them, and not with those who do not call on necessity but suffer it, and do not contribute to this evil, except in not wishing to perish at the whim of their enemies.

(d'Aubigné 1967: II, 86)

This view shows the recourse to arms as the consequence of a chain of events for which the Reformers have not been responsible. The *ferme* insists that only a relentless refusal to weaken will spare them further violence. The peace which the Bible advocates, he claims, will not result from a cowed and crushed Church. The narrator of

Le Caducée shows himself to be persuaded by the point of view of the *ferme*. D'Aubigné intimates by this that he himself considered that this approach alone could be reconciled with the Scriptures, despite its appearance of aggression. It is noteworthy, however, that he presents the point of view of the *ferme* at a distance, as it were, as if wishing it to be qualified in some way. Presumably he felt that assertion of armed strength was only appropriate to very particular circumstances.

A further pamphlet, *Traitté sur les guerres civiles*, written around 1625, seeks less to establish political justification for the defence of the Church than to rouse the reader to submit himself to the will of God in a situation in which he is physically threatened. The needs of the Church must supersede all private considerations, and any reluctance to respond to them would make men contemptible in the eyes of God:

> Qui est-ce encore de vous qui estime la froideur pour sagesse ou plus tost la tepidité qui vous feroit vomir de la bouche de Dieu?

> Who is there still amongst you that takes indifference for wisdom, or rather that lukewarm attitude which will cause you to be vomited from the mouth of god?
>
> (d'Aubigné 1967: II, 28)

Here the contempt of God is seen as far more important than the contempt of the enemy, with which the *ferme* in *La Caducée* was preoccupied. In this pamphlet, material victory is not regarded as important; it is the spiritual peril of failing to respond to God's will which is at stake. Because of this, d'Aubigné advocates willingness to fight for the Church even in the face of certain defeat. He argues that the victory which their enemies would claim, even if they succeeded in exterminating all the Protestants in France, would not really be a victory at all:

> quand ils auroyent exterminé & chassé de la France le dernier de nous, ils ne se peuvent vanter sinon que mille ont este victorieux sur un. Voila une violence de populace & du milieu duquel un soldat courageux se retireroit avec honte & horreur. Voila cette violence que je maintiens ne sentir le Chevalier, mais entierement le bourreau.

> when they have exterminated and chased out of France the last of us, they will be able to boast of nothing except that a thousand

have been victorious over one. This is violence of the people, from the midst of which a courageous soldier would withdraw with shame and horror. This is that violence which has nothing valiant about it, but smells entirely of the torturer.

(d'Aubigné 1967: II, 29)

This condemnation of butchery shows that d'Aubigné was revolted by the idea of gratuituous violence. What emerges in this pamphlet is his predominant concern with the spiritual perspective of the situation. The Reformers must not consider the mere physical proportions of their plight, but must see it as a challenge to their readiness to submit to what God has ordained. D'Aubigné makes a further important point in this pamphlet which was not mentioned in *Le Caducée*, except for the implications of the narrator's opening remarks: the centrality of the Reformers' own sin. D'Aubigné stresses that their sin has called for chastisement and that they must struggle to control it. When they no longer repel God through their sinfulness, all things will be granted to them:

> Toutes choses vous abonderont quand vos pechés n'eslogneront plus la face de Celuy qui a les victoires en sa main.

> All things will be granted to you when your sins no longer repel Him who has all victories in his hand.

(d'Augibné 1967: II, 32)

This insistance that the fundamental cause of their miseries was their own sin marks d'Aubigné out from the pamphleteers of the 1570s, writing after the massacre of St Bartholomew's Day, whose attitudes tended towards self-righteousness and venomous contempt for their enemies. Although the *Traitté sur les guerres civiles* refers the reader to the famous *Vindiciae contra Tyrannos* for the legal arguments for resistance, d'Aubigné is far more concerned with the will of God than with the rights of man.

Both *Le Caducée* and the *Traitté sur les guerres civiles* show expediency as a great moral enemy. *Le Caducée* demonstrates that the man of compromise is essentially self-indulgent. He is prepared to set aside consideration of the needs of the Church for mere self-protection. He is ready to accept a veneer of peace and to disregard realities. In the *Traitté*, the duress to which the Reformers were submitted is shown as part of a larger pattern of sin and chastisement, and this gives a metaphysical as well as a moral proportion to the struggle.

In d'Aubigné's letters the idea recurs that war is the consequence of sin and has been permitted to ensure the chastisement of man. An undated letter to M. Rohan speaks of war joining with famine and plague as instruments of God's wrath:

> Vous voyez, Monseigneur, quel est le visage de l'Europe entiere, espouvantable de 34 grandes armees, sur lesquelles le ciel gresle, et fait plus de meurtres justes qu'injustes: le couteau, la faim et la peste marchent au son des tambours, et font leurs charges plus souvent que les trompettes ne la sonnent.

> You see, my Lord, the face of Europe in its entirety, repulsive with its 34 great armies, on which the heavens let hail fall, and allow more just murders than unjust: the knife, hunger and plague march to the sound of the drums, and charge more often than the trumpets sound.

> (d'Aubigné 1967: I, 403)

War as a punishment for sin is acknowledged in a letter to his daughter, in which d'Aubigné writes: 'La calamité est partout, pour ce que le peché estoit partout' ('Calamity is everywhere, since sin was everywhere'). In the midst of this calamity, which sin has brought about, d'Aubigné reminds his acquaintances that their ability to retain their allegiance was a sign of grace. In a letter to M. de Montausier, d'Aubigné writes:

> Vous estes obligé de Dieu à vous ne lasser point en un siecle ou la verité est prisonniere ou bloquee de si prez par la diligence & l'autorite de ses ennemis, qu'elle n'a plus de commerce avec les humains que par les courages plus relevez qui percent les gardes posees contre elle par les rares exemples de leur magnanimité.

> You are indebted to God not to have abandoned you in an age in which truth is imprisoned or walled up by the concern and authority of its enemies, so that she no longer has any contact with humans except through souls of great courage which penetrate the shields held against her by the rare examples of their magnanimity.

> (d'Aubigné 1967: I, 382)

Although this statement reads as a eulogy of the qualities of the steadfast Reformers, fundamentally d'Aubigné set little store by human potential. Although steadfastness was a testimony to the power of grace, human qualities had no power to remedy the predicament that had led to the civil troubles. In an account of his meeting with Cardinal du Perron on a theological issue, d'Aubigné underlines the limitations of all human resources:

> apres un discours de sa facon sur les miseres des divisions, il me demanda comme gemissant si nous ne saurions faire quelque chose de bon. Je respondis que non, parce que nous n'etions pas bons.

> after a speech in his own fashion about the miseries of opposing views, he asked me in a trembling voice if we might do something good. I replied that we might not, since we were not good.
> (d'Aubigné 1967: I, 387)

All d'Aubigné's comments on political matters, both in his pamphlets and in his letters, are characterized by an awareness of the basic deficiencies of humanity. He even rejects the notion of looking to a human leader for guidance, stating in one letter that there was no merit in espousing the views of Luther or of Calvin: men would be judged by 'la seule credition qu'ils portent a la parole de Dieu' ('solely by the belief that they have in the word of God'). Although d'Aubigné was highly responsive to the political quandary of his time, the terms of human argument were not adequate for him to survey it. His concept of allegiance was indissolubly qualified by his acknowledgement of the deficiency of all human enterprise.

D'Aubigné did not underestimate the distress and perplexity of the man who was both victim and instigator of the troubles of his time. This state of misery is developed fully in his psalm meditations, where the plight of his co-religionaries serves as illustration of man's need of grace. He insists from the outset that he does not intend to stir political argument: 'Vous ne trouverez icy aucune piccoterie de nos controverses' ('You will find nowhere here any stirring of our present controversies'). On the other hand, he stresses that the circumstances of their composition had a strong bearing on the content. Indeed, he points out that the afflictions of his time are themselves indicative of a need for the word of God, since he is the only source of comfort 'en qui seul aux temps calamiteux se trouve conseil et consolation' ('in whom alone may counsel and consolation be found in times of calamity'). Calvin, in his preface to Bude's translation of the psalms, had shown how essential it was to concentrate on the Scriptures in order to avoid an exclusive preoccupation with the harrassment inflicted by men.

Mere mortal enemies had no importance compared with the threat of Satan himself. Both Calvin and d'Aubigné looked to the Scriptures for a point of reference which would serve as an infallible guide to the truth of the human condition. This alone would enable the afflicted Protestants to see beyond the particular features of their wretchedness and afford them an insight into the ultimate realities of their existence. Because of the centrality of the Scriptures in d'Aubigné's interpretation of experience, his psalm meditations are written in a very restrained way. In comparison with Sponde or de Bèze, who made a highly personal use of the freedom permissible in this genre, d'Aubigné relies almost exclusively on Biblical text for an expression of the positive assertions he wishes to make. However, for illustration of human weakness, he turns to the topical. A good example of this technique is to be found in his meditation on Psalm 73. It was written for the benefit of the former servants of Henri IV who considered themselves insufficiently rewarded for their endeavours. It is notable that d'Aubigné, who in many ways had an axe to grind about the treatment he received at the hands of his former master, does not plead their cause or boost their sense of worth. Indeed, he cites their resentment as an example of man's debility. He shows that to rebuke God in the face of the triumph of their enemies is an example of a common human failing, and that the sense of frustration and bitterness experienced by those who had seen no positive outcome to their labours was simply the sign of the inability of men to accept the reality which God had decreed: 'Le coeur humain est comme forcé de porter envie aux insensez, voyant la prosperité des meschans' ('The human heart is as though drawn to envy madmen, in view of the way the wicked prosper'). This resentment, he observes, is caused by an insistence on applying human standards of judgement, and by having no faith in the vaster judgement of God. The faithful must accept the adversity forced upon them, since it is a sign of God's will:

> Embrasse donc les afflictions les yeux au ciel, en disant: Quand tu me meurtrirois, si te beniroye; embrasse la mort, desireux de coeur & de bouche en sentent ces amertumes. Si est ce que Dieu est tres doux.

> Welcome afflictions, with your eyes raised to heaven, saying: When you destroy me, so shall I bless you. Welcome death,

willing to say with your heart and your voice, when you feel this bitter pain: So is God ever kind.

(d'Aubigné 1967: II, 156)

In his meditation on Psalm 16, d'Aubigné dismisses all human aspirations as illusions: 'Tous les desirs humains, voire les plus violens, sont trompeurs ou par le manquement ou par la satiete' ('All human desires, especially the most violent, are deceptive through their inadequacy or their excess'). It is clear that d'Aubigné was able to interpret the afflictions of his time as a form of spiritual blessing, but he stressed that it was only possible to establish this perspective if human impulses for material victory were suppressed. The temptation to resent the vicissitude of circumstance was basically a far greater threat than any physical peril, and this temptation was to be resisted. What emerges from these observations is that d'Aubigné was urging a form of acquiescence which, paradoxically, united with a willingness to expose oneself to physical danger by fighting to protect the freedom of the Church. The encouragement to acquiesce to God's will expressed in the psalm meditations complements the directive to fight in the political pamphlets.

It is possible, therefore, to see that the militancy habitually ascribed to d'Aubigné needs to be qualified by an awareness of his vision of a universal spiritual predicament. This plight was of far more importance to him than the outcome of battles. The bloodshed and devastation of warfare are portrayed in his writing more as a sign of God's wrath with sinful humanity than as an instigation to more aggressive exploits. In his great poem *Les Tragiques* the presentation of war confirms this view. It is a lamentation of war, in which the reader's emotions are called on to acknowledge the full horror that human sin has brought about. In *Les Tragiques* war appears as an image of the self-destructiveness of sin. There is neither excitement nor bloodlust in d'Aubigné's account; we are shown a picture of misery and degradation. Based on a theological argument which shows man as essentially trapped in the consequences of his sin, the poem draws on the events of d'Aubigné's time to illustrate this theme, very much as topical elements appear in the psalm meditations to highlight the wisdom of the Bible. *Les Tragiques* also relies heavily on the Bible to establish a deep structure, and the evil and folly of the human condition are expressed by a demonstration of the havoc they have caused in late sixteenth-century France. A devotional treatment of this theme is developed in the poem, which, as well as deploring the sin which ravages the country, also laments it as a source of personal and communal guilt. Whereas Sponde and Chassignet, for example, were concerned with their own sin, d'Aubigné laments a more collective sin, but one with which he personally identifies. This ability to write both in his own name and in the name of all men is an aspect of the uniqueness of the poem.

Several features of the poem demonstrate its devotional perspective. D'Aubigné is able to exploit the familiar landscape of devastation to provide images of the sin which he wishes at the same time to confess and to condemn. The tone of much of these sections is one of penitential anguish, insisting on the ugliness of the communal identity, which is also very much his own:

Au lieu de Thessalie aux mignardes vallees
Nous avortons ces chants au milieu des armees,
En delassant nos bras de crasse tous rouillez
Qui n'osent s'esloigner des brassards despouillez.

Instead of in the lovely valleys of Thessalie, these songs are aborted in the midst of armies, relaxing our arms
thick with filth which do not dare distance themselves from the armfuls they have stolen.

(L.T.: Misères: 69)

He describes his muse as a figure of despair. She shrieks, rising from freshly dug graves:

bramant en la sorte
Que faict la biche apres le fan qu'elle a perdu.

moaning in the way
That a female deer lows after she has lost her fawn.

(L.T.: Misères: 69)

The poem is designed to create an aesthetic shock, contriving to create distasteful images to express the ugliness of sin. Just as Desportes in his devotional poetry described with revulsion the effects of sickness on his body, d'Aubigné uses similar graphic details of sickness to appall his readers, but generalizes the plight. He creates an image of the whole of France as a diseased monster, displaying all the repulsive features of the ailing human:

La masse degenere en la melancholie
Ce vieil corps, tout infect, plein de sa discrasie
Hydropique, fait l'eau, si bien que ce geant
Qui allait de ses nerfs ses voisins outrageant
Aussi foible que grand n'enfle plus que son ventre.

The mass degenerates into melancholia
This aged body, all diseased, bulging with hydropic
disorder, produces water alone, so that the giant
who, with the great nervous strength outraged her
neighbours, is now as weak as she is huge, and only
her stomach swells.

(L.T.: Misères: 145)

The image of the sick giant conveys the imbalance of life created
by the disorder of human disobedience. Another devotional theme,
which links up with that of sickness, is of course death, and it is
above all through his portrait of death that d'Aubigné is able to
characterize the full horror of sin. Death is revealed in *Les Tragiques*
as the only fruit of sin. *Misères* and *Les Fers* (the first and fifth books
of the poem) contain extensive descriptions of the dead and dying.
Death is not presented here as a reminder of the moribund nature
of the individual, but acts as an image of the dissipation of the
whole country. The origin and the consequences of the horror are
similarly frightful. D'Aubigné creates a distressing picture of a
town left desolate by mercenaries:

La de mille maisons on ne trouva que feux,
Que charongnes, que morts ou visages affreux.

In the place where a thousand houses stood,
we found only fire, only corpses, only the dead,
or appalling faces.

(L.T.: Misères: 379)

In a ransacked house, there is a dying family. Highly emotive
language describes the mother as she vainly tries to nourish her
child; d'Aubigné presents her as an image of France:

ce corps seché retraict,
De la France qui meurt fut un autre portaict.

> this withered, dried out body
> presented another image of France in the grip of death.
>
> (L.T.: Misères: 423)

Without an understanding of the religious structure of the poem, descriptions such as these might well appear as sentimental outbursts. However, d'Aubigné has chosen with great care aspects of his country's plight that suggest not merely a physical but a spiritual quandary. The ugliness and wretchedness of the people and the landscape which he surveys are evoked to portray the fundamental nature of humanity. In this way, war and its consequences are shown as the outward signs of the way in which sin has overcome man.

D'Aubigné's presentation of war is markedly different in all the genres that have been discussed. But, although the perspectives are different, the fundamental issue with which his writings are concerned remains the same. Physical warfare is not d'Aubigné's preoccupation. He writes consistently about sin, its causes and its effects. Only the axiom of God's glory and the folly of men can make sense of his *Histoire Universelle,* and so greatly does he trust the clarity of the axiom that in this work he describes warfare without emotion. In his pamphlets he is anxious to present the moral issues of the predicament in which the Reformers found themselves, showing the relation of circumstance to the challenge of God's will. The psalm meditations are more concerned with the inner realities of the soul, and show how the force of circumstances had been able to imperil the spiritual integrity of the Reformers. *Les Tragiques* laments man's wretchedness and shows how his sin has been the source of his chastisement. D'Aubigné's treatment of war is designed to illustrate the helplessness of man without God. War and its effects provide an outstanding example of the negative nature of the human condition since, left to their own resources, men could only worsen their plight. By looking to the conflicts of his time, d'Aubigné found a means of expressing the depravity of the human condition. His presentation of war asserts the same truth as Calvin's comment:

> Car qu'est ce que tu as de toy-mesme, sinon peché?
> Si tu veux prendre ce qui est tien, prend le peché,
> car la iustice est de Dieu.

What do you have of your own, except sin?
If you wish to have what is yours, take sin,
for justice is of God.

(I.C.: II. II. 11)

Chapter 3

Resistance justified

THE PAMPHLETEERS' ACCOUNT

It is clear from d'Aubigné's pamphlets, as well as from the desolation of *Les Tragiques*, that the position of entrenched militancy which the Reformers had increasingly been compelled to adopt was to d'Aubigné a source of horror rather than of glory. He shows them as trapped within the demands of 'la seule necessite'; stating, in other words, that they had no choice: the need to fight had been imposed by God. D'Aubigné would have agreed with the militant Reformers that the Royalist attempt to stifle their worship was a challenge to their loyalty to God: it was to be resisted. However, whereas d'Aubigné saw this necessity as a tragic consequence of man's inherent inability to organize and to control his existence, several other Reformers found in it a clear pointer to their own superiority. It gave them a sense of being a spiritual elite. In their writing, there is an absence of any self-rebuke. This separation between a consciousness of a general sinfulness and a conviction of the favour of God marked the beginnings of a 'Calvinism' (see Hill 1973: 206), which was to form the basis of subsequent thinking of men who opposed their rulers on moral grounds. It was, however, far from Calvin's own thought.

The seditious potential of the Reformers' thought had by now developed fully and the pamphlets of the 1570s asserted that the monarchy of Charles IX was a tyrannical power, which contravened the word of God. The 'Monomachs' have been extensively studied for the political content of their approach, which subsequently offered scope for many movements keen to justify their resistance to their ruler (see Kelley 1991). Submission before such rulers, it was argued, would lead to the erosion of all Christian values:

> Nous ne doutons point que l'enseignement de l'Apostre qui dit: 'Faites bien a tous' ne s'estende iusques aux plus grands ennemis que nous ayons: mais aussi nous disons que ce mot de tous doit estre prins en sa propre signification afin que ne mettions vice pour vertu, cruauté pour humanité, & mensonge pour verité.

> We do not doubt that the teaching of the Apostle, which states 'do good to all' extends to the worst enemies that we have: but also we maintain that the world 'all' must be taken at its true meaning, so that we do not take vice for virtue, cruelty for humanity, and lies for truth.
>
> (Goulard 1578: II, 260)

Such pamphlets were intended to clear the Reformers of the moral responsibility of starting the wars. The following is a good example of the kind of argument that presented the Reformers as a purifying force:

> En toutes choses il y a deux sortes de cause, les unes sont internes et substantielles de la chose. Il y a d'autres causes exterieures et accidentales. Nous nions donc que notre doctrine soit cause des guerres civiles en la seconde espece des choses peut estre cause des guerres. Tout ainsi que l'homme qui nettoye une fontaine pourra estre dit cause d'avoir troublé la fontaine. Mais la corruption et la cause interieure est es ordures qui y estoient. Car par accident il a falu qu'il l'ait troublé pour le nettoier. . . . Concluons donc que la cause des guerres en France n'est pas L'Evangile ni en ceux qui font profession d'iceluy.

> In all things there are two sorts of cause, some are interior and substantial to the thing itself. There are other causes, which are external and which are accidental. We deny, therefore, that our doctrine is the cause of the civil wars, in the second sense. Just as a man who has cleaned a fountain may not be said to have disturbed the fountain. However, the corruption and the intrinsic cause was in the filth there already. It was accidental that the man had to disturb the water in order to cleanse it. . . . We may thus conclude that the cause of the wars in France is not in the Holy Gospel, nor in those who uphold it.
>
> (Goulard 1578: II, 240)

This kind of argument demonstrates well how the Reformers felt compelled to interpret the situation in polarized moral terms. We find also in pamphlets of this period the rejection of the monarch when he no longer is seen to uphold his responsibilities towards the people:

> C'est merveille que de tous temps les suiets ayent este si soigneux de garder leurs droicts: les Roys si raisonnables de ne demander ny pretendre que ce que leur appartient en choses simplement civiles et politiques. Et que nous aujourd'huy soyons si hors du sens d'oser dire, ou croire que la justice & le pur service ce Dieu puissent & doivent estre reglez & compassez a la fantasisie d'un seul homme mortel, lequel selon qu'il sera mené de diverses passions, se permettra gouverner le ciel et la terre . . .

> It is amazing that at all times the subjects of the realm have been so careful to conserve their rights: the kings so reasonable as not to demand nor to claim anything beyond what belonged to them as far as civil and political issues were concerned. And that, today, we are so unreasonable as to say, or to believe that justice and the pure service of God might and should be ruled and circumscribed by the whim of one mortal man alone, who, according to the way in which his various passions affect him, will take on the rule of both heaven and earth . . .
>
> (Goulard 1578: II, 255)

The priorities established long before by Luther and by Calvin and clarified by de Bèze, in terms of their implications for the demands of a threat to the Church within society, now find a new emphasis. At the point where the prince no longer fulfils his role in the terms established by God, he no longer has authority:

> Les peuples respondent, Nous ne recognoissons apres Dieu que nostre prince, tant pour l'obligation que pour le devoir naturel, et nous honorons sa personne et observerons ses edits; mais nous avons l'injure, la terreur, l'outrage, l'hostilite ordinairement a nos costez, et ceux que se disent nos protocteure nous devorent. Par ainsi ne nous sert de rien le nom de paix publique, puisqu'en particulier on nous fait sentir l'effect et l'aigreur de la guerre. Ce glaive donc donne de Dieu est pour [en] faire justice.

> The people reply, after God we recognize our prince alone, as

much through obligation as natural duty, and we honour his person and will observe his laws: but we find aggression, terror, outrage and hostility around us at all times, and those who call themselves our protectors devour us. In this way, the term 'public peace' means nothing to us, because we ourselves are made to feel the impact and bitterness of war. God has laid down this challenge to demand justice.

(Goulard 1578: III, 63)

One discerns in this type of argument a degree of self-protection and a concern with the discomfort of immediate experience which are already far from Calvin's insistence on a commitment to God's will totally regardless of self. Barnaud's *Dialogue auquel sont traitées plusieurs Choses advenues aux Luthériens et Huguenots de la France* illustrates how politics, in the sense of deliberate calculated organization, has gained esteem in the eyes of the Reformers. Barnaud relates a discussion between the Church, the Spirit of Truth (Athylie), the Friend of Truth, 'Seigneur Politique' and a Historian. The Friend of Truth arrives in France accompanied by the Historian and by 'Seigneur Politique'. The Spirit of Truth is at first suspicious at the presence of 'Seigneur Politique':

Je suis plus aise de te voir accompagné de l'un que de l'autre, sçachant combien l'un est necessaire et profitable pour aider à la memoire, et servir à la posterité: et l'autre, le plus souvent pernicieux et dommageable, principalent s'il est nourri à la cour d'aucuns Rois et Princes que tu cognois bien.

I am more at ease to see you accompanied by the first rather than the second, knowing how the former is so necessary and useful to help our memory and to serve posterity, and the latter so often pernicious and harmful, especially if he is brought up in the court of certain Kings and Princes whom you know very well.

(Barnaud 1573: 1)

However, after the narration of the events of St Bartholomew's Day, Truth admonishes 'Seigneur Politique' for taking so little action:

Je m'esmerveille grandement, Seigneur Politique Francois, considerant le piteux estat de la France (si tu as ta patrie en quelque recommendation) maintenant qu'elle a plus de besoin de ses vrais amis bons conseillers qu'elle ne'eut oncques, comme c'est que tu as eu le courage de l'abandonner: au lieu de t'employer à guerir sa playe, à la penser, de la frenesie et de la rage qui la meine.

I am greatly amazed, Lord French Politics, considering the pitiful state of France (if you hold your fatherland in some consideration) and now that she has more than at any time need of real good friends and counsellors, that you had the gall to abandon her, instead of busying yourself to heal her wound, and to cure her of the frenzy and rage which have taken her over.

(Barnaud 1573: 95)

'Seigneur Politique' is advised to muster friends and supporters throughout France without delay, and to do all within his power not only to glorify God but to conserve as many Reformers as possible.

All these considerations, the logical analysis, the emphasis on self-preservation, the upgrading of political involvement, suggest a major departure from Calvin's attitude. Calvin had asserted that no rule could be so despotic as to eclipse all justice, because God's will always lay behind the institution of that rule:

Nous devons tant estimer l'ordre de Dieu qu'il nous convient meme d'honorer les tyrans qui ont la domination; et qu'il n'y eut jamais, et on ne peut songer a une tyrannie si cruelle et debordée en laquelle il ne paraisse quelqu'espece d'equité.

We must so far respect the order established by God that we must even honour the tyrants who rule; there has never been and we may not conceive a tyranny which is so cruel and extreme that it does not contain some form of equity.

(Lagarde 1926: 234)

Languet, however, in the *Vindiciae*, saw tyranny as an inevitable precursor to sedition. In his view, the tyrant has usurped the natural contract whereby he can only expect subservience from the people if he is himself subservient to God. He no longer has rights to his kingdom:

Au cas semblable le Roy perd de droit, et quelquefois de fait son Royaume, s'il mesprise Dieu, s'il complotte avec les ennemis d'iceluy, et s'il comet felonie contre Dieu.

In such a case, the King loses the right to his Kingdom, and sometimes the Kingdom itself, if he despises God, if he plots with his enemies and commits a felony against God.

(Languet 1581: 24)

The prince who contravenes the laws of God is as guilty of 'lèse-majesté' as any rebellious vassal, Languet claims, and the people have no duty whatsoever to obey him:

> comme les serviteurs ne sont tenus d'obéir a leurs maistres, s'ils commandent quelquechose contra la volonte de Dieu: les suiets pareillement ne doyvent obéissance aux Rois qui leur veulent faire outre-passer la loy de Dieu.

> just as servants are not obliged to obey their masters if they order something which contravenes the will of God, so subjects owe no obedience to rulers who wish them to exceed God's law.

(Languet 1581: 24)

It is up to the people, affirms Languet, to restore order, and he makes it clear that by the people he means the magistrates entrusted by the Reformed Church to ensure the moral integrity of secular organization. Languet concentrates on the possibility of a political solution to the situation and implies that the disintegration of the social order that has followed the prince's tyrannical behaviour can be rectified through human resources. He treats with scorn those Reformers who still worry about the legitimacy of open rebellion against the monarch:

> Certains garnemens objectent qu'es choses mesmes qui concernent la conscience il faut obeir aux Rois et sont effrontez iusques la de produire pour tesmoins d'une opinion si meschante les Apostres S Pierre et S Paul.

> Ayant aujourd'hui à faire à ennemis qui sont sans humanité et sans foy, et tous remplis de trahison et de cruauté, ne prennant plaisir qu'a respandre le sang innocent de guet a pens iusques à ce qu'ils ayent mis a mort tous les fideles: nous disons en tel cas que qui veut user du droit naturel, humain et divin, il faut mettre à mort telle manière de gens.

> Some wretches maintain that even in matters concerning the conscience, kings must be obeyed, and are as bold as to present

as witnesses to such a wicked opinion the Apostles St Peter and St Paul.

Having today to deal with enemies who have neither humanity, nor faith and who all are filled with treason and cruelty, taking pleasure only in spilling innocent blood until they have put all the faithful to death; we say that in such a case to anyone who wishes to apply natural law both human and divine, such people must be killed.

(Languet 1581: 43–4)

It is notable that the collective identity of the Reformers asserted in these pamphlets is expressed defensively; there is no suggestion that human sin in general is responsible for the miseries of war. From their point of view, the situation in which they saw themselves persecuted had assumed epic proportions. The contemporary observer saw the Reformers' unity as their most impressive feature. Michel de l'Hôpital remarked:

Ce ne sont pas genz ramassez, comme on a mis en avant depuis peu de jours, esmeuz et souslevez par imprudence, sans ordre sans chef et sans discipline; ce sont genz agguerez, resoleuz, reduicts au desespoir; et pourtant se tenant collez et conjoinctz ensemble, sans endurer qu'on les desunisse par moyens et artifices quelconques; Comme de ceste liaison et union despendent la seureté et repoz de leurs vies, maisons, femmes, enfants, honneurs et estatz, se tiennent fermes en une resolution de mourir tous ensemble plutost de subir le joug de leurs ennemys.

These are not people who, as has been claimed, were raised up recently, bolstered and pushed on by rashness, without order, without leader and without discipline; these are men prepared for war, resolved, reduced to despair; nevertheless, standing close and united, allowing no one to sever them by any means or artifice. As on this link and unity the safety and peace of their lives, their houses, wives and children, their honour and their property depend, they remain firm in a resolution rather to die together than to submit to the yoke of their enemies.

(Michel de l'Hôpital 1822–6: II, 177)

Identification with the tribe of Israel reinforced the communal spirit but would appear to have undermined the interiority of Calvin's counsel of self-doubt.

Indeed, one cannot see in the arguments expressed in the pamphlets of the period following the outbreak of hostilities in the civil wars any evidence that self-doubt and human inadequacy survived in the minds of these Reformers as focal points of consideration. One might say that these pamphlets were not in themselves a development of Calvin's thought but amounted to a side-stepping of its central themes. Quite clearly, it was possible for arguments against the intrinsic moral authority of monarch or magistrate to be found in Calvin's writing. But to isolate the condemnation of a corrupt authority was to misrepresent the general tenor of Calvin's theology. The most striking difference between the militant pamphlets of the 1570s and Calvin's writing is one of tone. In the *Institution Chrestienne*, his biblical commentaries and his pamphlets, Calvin's prose has an underlying gravity, which prevails especially when he demonstrates the irony of human self-justification. The style of Languet and Barnaud tends to be derisive and even facetious; their scorn is not of human nature in general, but of opposition to their own stance. It asserts a brash self-confidence, and an apparent conviction that the use of arms can set matters right. There is no trace of lament for the consequences of a common sin, but a placing of blame uniquely on the shoulders of those who have troubled the Reformers.

A POET'S ACCOUNT

The epic poem of Du Bartas, *La Judit*, written between 1566 and 1574, reflects quite distinctly the advocation of resistance to tyrants set forth in the militant pamphlets quoted above. Although in some ways the tone of this poem, recounting Judith's murder of the tyrant Holofernes, is more dignified than the derisive idiom of the pamphlets, the content provides the same message. It is interesting that Du Bartas' advocation of tyrannicide is not the only element of his work which departs from Calvin's precepts: he also makes adjustments to the criteria which Calvin defines as appropriate for the artist to adopt, in the light of the spiritual priorities of the Reformed faith. The passionate tone of the narrative of *La Judit* is inconsistent with Calvin's statement that the artist should use his talent soberly, tempered with a recollection of man's inadequacy. In the *Institution Chrestienne*, Calvin wrote:

Il y danger de reculer bien loin de l'usage saint et legitime des dons de Dieu. . . . Il faudra en user avec pure conscience. Quand ils [i.e. artists] aurant reduit leurs coeurs a cette sobriete, ils auront la regle de bon usage.

There is a danger in departing too far from the holy and legitimate use of the gifts of God. . . . They must be employed with a clear conscience. When they [i.e. artists] have disposed their hearts to this sober intention, then they will have found the rules appropriate to their art.

(I.C.: II. II. 14)

Calvin warned against flattering 'les passions humaines', and condemned disorder and exaggeration. Principally, Calvin encouraged the writer to humble himself before his imitation of God's work and to present a balanced view of his subject in all simplicity and without pride. Ultimately the subject matter and not the skill in representation would decide the value of the artist's achievement. Above all, Calvin recommended that the writer should turn to the Bible for his criterion of appropriate expression and of truth.

An examination of *La Judit* shows that Du Bartas was not primarily concerned with seeking to express Calvin's priorities in the field of artistic endeavour, and neither was he out to offer a theological interpretation of the events of the story of Judith's assassination of Holofernes that would be consistent with Calvin's thought. Although the poem takes a Biblical theme as its basis, Du Bartas relies on the Bible very little and does not hesitate to suppress as well as to add to the Apocryphal book which provided his source. There is much in the poem which, both in tone and argument, links it with the writing of Protestant pamphleteers of the 1570s.

Joachim, in the *Livre Premier* of the poem, rallies his fellow princes in a language evocative of the Protestant zeal of the 1570s, urging them to resist the tyrant. He is opposed by a 'traistre viellard', who argues that it might well be advantageous to humble themselves before the tyrant and he would then be indulgent towards them. To rise against him with 'indiscrete zele' might well lead to the annihilation of the house of Jacob. Significantly, the traitor claims that they have free will to decide their own fate: 'Puis que donc nous pouvons ore elire pour nous/La guerre ou le repos . . .' ('Since we may choose for ourselves war or rest . . .') (Du Bartas 1974: I, 251–2). Even without Du Bartas's mention of the black bile seething from the mouth and stomach of the speaker, the Reformers of the period would have understood that he was reasoning along unsound lines and that the Israelites were being advised to put the tyrant before their God. Such an attitude was denounced vehemently in Languet's *Vindiciae contra Tyrannos*: the whim of the tyrant must be treated with contempt and the word of God alone must rule. Languet portrays the readiness to acquiesce for the sake of peace as sheer cowardice:

> Concluons de cela qu'il faut acquiescer a tout ce que le Roy ordonnera, et embrasser sans replique telle superstition qu'il lui plaira d'establir. Mais il n'y a homme tant soit-il grossier qui ne voye l'ineptie et impieté de telles gens . . .

> Let us derive from this view that it is essential to acquiesce before everything the King might command, and to embrace without demur any superstitious whim that it might please him to impose. But there is no man so gross that he does not see the stupidity and impiety of such a view.
>
> (Languet (?) 1581: 34)

In the third book of *La Judit* more echoes of militant Reformers' preoccupations are to be found. Many of the Israelites lose heart at the prospect of combat with Holofernes and their zeal evaporates. At this point, Du Bartas spells out the parallel with his own day, intervening directly into the narrative:

> He! combien voyons-nous de tels Ephraimites
> En ce temps malheureux, qui vivent, ypocrites,
> Dans l'Eglise tandis qu'un zephyre clement
> Contre sa saincte pouppe haleine heureusement
> Et d'un zele farde embrassent l'Evangile.

> How many such Ephraimites
> Do we see in these unhappy times,
> Who live as hypocrites within the Church whilst
> A clement wind breathes happily on her holy prow,
> And with a false zeal embrace the Gospel.
>
> (Du Bartas 1974: 3, 61–5)

The subsequent siege of Bethulie provides an opportunity for Du Bartas to cite the great source of consolation which sustained the Reformers during the troubles of the civil wars: God delays coming to the aid of his people only to impose even greater punishment in the end.

The encouragement to oppose tyrannic rule with arms recalls quite markedly the militant pamphlets of Du Bartas's time. The editor of the latest edition of *La Judit* claims that Du Bartas is advocating tyrannicide in his poem (Du Bartas 1974: 42). Such an approach runs directly against Calvin's counsel of patience.

However, the theological strain of *La Judit* is not exclusively militant. Many features of it do in fact cohere with Calvin's theology. The emptiness of human expediency is a theme which Calvin stressed, and this emphasis is expressed in Judith's admonition to the governor of the city once he is persuaded to abandon the siege:

> vous voules donc limiter la puissance
> Du Pere tout-puissant et captiver ses mains
> Dans les fresles chainons de vos conseils humains?

> do you thus wish to limit the power of almighty
> God, and to tie his hands in the frail chains of
> human counsel?

(Du Bartas 1974: 3, 456–8)

Judith's action in killing Holofernes provides the poem with a dimension which displays the power of God intervening to relieve human misery. Although in fact the account of Judith's courage and her calculated tactics has sustained much of the narrative, Du Bartas is anxious to point out that the work is God's alone:

> O Dieu, que dextrement ta saincte providence
> Renverse les desseings de l'humaine prudence!
> Car pour guider l'esleu au salut destine,
> Quand mesme il en est plus, comme il semble, esloigné
> Tu tires bien du mal . . .

> O God, how skilfully your holy providence
> Defeats the design of human prudence!
> For, in order to guide the elect to the destiny of salvation,
> even if he is, as it seems, further away from it than ever,
> You draw good from evil . . .

(Du Bartas 1974: 6, 183–7)

The story from the Apocrypha is cleverly dramatized by Du Bartas. Although references to Calvin's theology are detectable, their importance lies in the stimulus they provide to the reader's response;

they do not cohere to make a statement. Above all there are clearly affinities with contemporary militant literature which reject Calvin's recommendation that man should concentrate principally on his own sinfulness and endure all affliction with patience. In the 1581 edition, Du Bartas took the precaution of warning his readers against the assumption that they might launch into a physical attack on their rulers: 'Il me suffira pour ce coup d'admonester le lecteur de n'attenter rien sans une clair et indubitable vocation sur la vie de ceux que Dieu a esleves sur nous' ('It will suffice me for the moment to warn the reader not to make any attempt on the life of those whom God has raised above us without a clear and indisputable sense of vocation') (Du Bartas 1974: Preface, 4). He was clearly aware of the identity of the readers to whom he wished to appeal and the topical themes which he weaves into his narrative help to enhance its emotive impact. The arguments which evoke the Reformers' militancy are used principally to characterize; the voice of the author occasionally makes a direct contribution to underline the moral lesson of events, but there is no evidence to suggest that the poem was designed to work out a personal stance towards its subject matter. It would seem rather to aim at relating a tale in the most vivid and dramatic way possible. The distance that Du Bartas keeps from the Bible suggests that he was anxious to conserve an independence for poetic reasons; in his preface to the 1581 edition he states with some pride that he has used the Bible to provide an historical basis for the poem, but that the work's most significant merit lay in its skilful imitation of Homer and Virgil.

Du Bartas seems to have sought above all to delight on an emotive and on an aesthetic level. The description of Judith's beauty in the Petrarchan tradition, for example, adds a dimension of sensual pleasure quite irrelevant to any moral lesson. The description of the violence inflicted on Holofernes's head by the Israelites would appear to satisfy a desire to read about an excessively sadistic revenge. Any elements of Calvin's theology which the poem reflects are undermined by its principal theme of the need to slay the tyrant.

Different ideas of resistance emerge from the writers considered so far. Calvin's concern with the spiritual welfare of the inner man expresses above all the need to fight an interior battle, against willing complicity with sin. In order to be victorious in this battle, humility is the only resource possible. Man must admit that he contains within himself the sin which makes his life worthless. As St Augustine had written, the man who turns towards himself turns away from God.

D'Aubigné's work represents an effort to acknowledge this sin, both in himself and in his co-religionaries. He treats his own experience as a prime example of the folly of man and the strength of God: the account of it that he offers is aimed to share with his readers the truth that he has discovered. This truth is essentially of God; and is expressed for all time in the Bible. For this reason, quotations from the Bible provide a coherent structure to his work. The account of the unrest of his time exemplifies the incoherence of man. The writing of the pamphleteers and the poem of Du Bartas are based on self-assertion; the pamphleteers express no interiority other than a confidence in their own justification. Du Bartas is concerned with his poetic skill to rouse a partisan readership. These writers are involved in pleasing readers who have already decided their political affiliation.

It has been said that the Monomachs wrote in a way that advanced the formation of a political stance of resistance. Calvin and d'Aubigné were concerned with an inner paradox, which demanded self-effacement before any spiritual advance could be made.

Chapter 4

From Calvin to Cromwell through Beard

The image of Oliver Cromwell which survives today is unclear: in many ways it is self-contradictory. He is remembered as a successful military leader, as an ambitious acquisitor of power. But also he is identified with an attitude loosely termed 'Puritanism', which is largely understood as a suspicion of man's unhedged appetites, and an insistence on total deference to the will of God. The views held of Cromwell by his contemporaries were no less irreconcilable. As early as 1647, his former friend John Lilburne was accusing him of a betrayal of his pledge to campaign for civil liberties; his private attempt to draw up an agreement with the king suggested an exclusive interest in advancing his own ambition (see Gregg 1986: 191). Literally at the same time, Joshua Sprigge wrote on the achievements of the New Model Army, stating that Cromwell was clearly a man singled out by providence, which had designed him for the greater good of the kingdom (see Morrill 1990: 262). Then, as now, Cromwell's behaviour appeared obscure in motivation.

It has been possible to interpret his priorities differently. To some, these appear pragmatic, if not hypocritical. Cromwell was no intellectual, no theologian. He did not write copiously in order to furnish an apology for his response to the challenges of his time in power. However, his letters and speeches recurrently indicate certain features of his outlook which illuminate his understanding of his responsibilities and also of his inner identity.

It is well known that Cromwell never attached himself to any particular religious sect. Along with the Parliamentarians of the 1640s, he was committed to 'defend protestantism' together with 'the power and privileges of parliament' (Hill 1986: 7). Royal supremacy and episcopal power aroused the resentment of many of the English, who, by 1641, were widely conversant with the

Bible. Christopher Hill writes that 'religion was common discourse and table talk in every tavern and ale house' (Hill 1977: 97). Milton was able to formulate the reason for this sense of the restriction implied by a Laudian form of religion. In the *De Doctrina Christiana*, Milton declared that the Reformation in England had not been a great turning point; 'religion has been defiled with impurities for more than 1300 years', he wrote (Milton 1953: VI, 117). For Milton, the challenge was evident: the English must be freed from the servile fear which the bishops imposed on them. Cromwell entered parliament at this time and in this climate, but there is no evidence that he consciously analysed the moral issues at stake himself. However, a very early letter to his cousin, Mrs St John, in 1638, shows how passionately Cromwell was willing to commit himself to a cause which he could identify as a cause of God's will:

> My soul is the congregation of the first born, my body rests in hope, and if here I may honour my God either by doing or by suffering, I shall be most glad. Truly, no poor creature hath more cause to put forward himself in the cause of God than I
>
> (Abbott: I, 97)

The desire to honour God by doing or by suffering was to Cromwell a powerful motivation for service in the parliamentary army, in which he was active from 1642 onwards. However, this statement to his cousin alone gives little insight into the vital priorities which were to affect Cromwell's actions throughout his life and give rise to responses which, then as now, are hard to understand. The notion that a military triumph might be seen as tribute to God needs investigation.

For the time in which Cromwell was fighting, the term Calvinist is unspecific. Certainly a change had taken place between Calvin's terms of understanding the human condition, and those developed by the later Calvinists in France, who were directly involved in political challenge. The way in which the spiritual priorities of Calvin were adjusted in the course of the development of Puritanism in England has been much discussed (see Lamont 1969). Throughout this period, debate continued as to what value might be ascribed to human endeavour. The watered-down version of Calvinism which survived in England echoed Calvin's suspicion of human motivation, yet suggested that to be aware of God's providence indicated that salvation had already been achieved. From this viewpoint, the notion of the Godly emerged, the man who was totally committed to God's will, yet ready and able to co-operate with it.

An interesting exponent of this attitude is found in the work of Thomas Beard, Cromwell's tutor from 1604, when he was appointed master at the free school in Huntingdon. He was later to prepare Cromwell for entrance to Sidney Sussex College.

Before his appointment at Cambridge, Beard published in 1597 a book called *The Theatre of God's Judgements*, allegedly translated from the French. The French texts to which he was indebted are difficult to establish: the 1648 edition mentions de Bèze, Nicholas Gilles, Enguerra de Mostrel and Languet Chronica as 'authors from whom the most part of the examples contained in this book are collected'. The citing of these writers alone, however, indicates the climate of thought which influenced Beard, and which his own work develops. The way in which the French Reformers immediately involved in political challenge altered Calvin's emphasis from the polarization between God and man to an active response to the demands of God's will is reflected in Beard's book.

Beard's work here is directed towards the active rather than to the contemplative response. Although the book purports to be an account of the various points at which God has intervened in human affairs, its impact is designed to awaken in the reader a consciousness of his own moral identity. The basis of this awareness must derive from an acknowledgement of God's presence in immediate event:

> nothing in the world cometh to pas by chance or adventure but only and alwaies by the prescription of his will
>
> (Beard 1631: 2)

Like Calvin, Beard stresses the basic incomprehensibility of God's wisdom; however, equally like Calvin, he saw history as a source of revelation. A reminder of this perspective served to discourage a pragmatic approach to history, which might suggest that the conflicts between men could be resolved in human terms alone. This approach to history, stressing its metaphysical significance, served also to focus on immediate event: this too should be seen in the light of God's will, and not of human self-interest.

The emphasis of Beard's presentation of history and of contemporary examples of the working of God's will is on the benefit a man may reap personally by acting on it. Through its lesson, it is possible to identify true values. We can understand that

to eschew vice, we must learn what vice and vertue is, and to
discerne the evil and the good which either of them bring forth,
to the end to beware lest we dash ourselves unaware against vice
instead of vertue and be caught with the deceitful traits thereof.

(Beard 1631: 2)

The terms of this moral lesson imply in the individual a capacity
for identifying and acting on the good. This approach was at a
considerable distance from Calvin, who would have insisted that,
through his own resources, man could not discern true good, and
certainly was unable to act on it through the operation of his own
will. According to Beard, awareness of the terms of God's will as
revealed by history can show men that good behaviour invited
God's favour:

whereby to learne to containe ourselves within the bounds of
modestie and the feare of God in seeing that they which have
carried themselves anything in equity, temperance and other
natural vertues, have been in some sort spared

(Beard 1631: 5)

The insight afforded to the faithful Christian through an awareness
of God's immediate intervention into human affairs gives him
considerable advantages, in Beard's view. Unlike the human being
described in Calvin's writing, and in that of d'Aubigné, irrevocably
severed from God by his very nature, Beard presents a privileged
existence, wherein life is a constant response to the presence of
God's manifest will, and a communication with it:

the faithful Christian may take occasion much more to acknowledge the great mercie and singular favour of God toward them,
in that they are renewed to a better conversation of life than
others.

(Beard 1631: 7)

The word 'conversation' suggests an almost Erasmian ability to
handle the terms of the divine. However, Beard does not overlook
the effects of original sin, which he portrays as devastating, when
unabated by God's grace, or by human effort to curb it. He describes how men in this state

not restrained by any bridle, like untamed colts broke loose, give
full swing to their bold and violent affections

(Beard 1631: I, 2)

Such men 'exercise these their natures by outrageious practices'. The picture Beard paints of unbridled man in society shows him completely dominated by self-interest. This causes widespread injustice:

> In this poor and miserable estate every man rocketh himself asleepe, and flattereth his owne humor, everie man pursueth his accustomed course of life, with an obstinate mind to do evill; yea, many of those that have power and authoritie over others, according as they are endowed and persuaded with a foolish conceit of themselves make themselves believe, that for them everything is lawful, and that they may do whatever they please . . .
>
> (Beard 1631: 5)

These men have condemned themselves to moral chaos, unable to identify any truth. The absence of stable values Beard attributes to this mentality is reminiscent of the way in which d'Aubigné described the intrinsic state of the human condition; its moral disorder was to him endemic. For him, as for Calvin, human resources are inadequate to establish any consistent point of reference. Beard, though, sees this confusion as an aspect of men who have no concept of social order:

> men speak evill of good, and good of evill, accounting darkness light and light darkness, sower sweet and sweet sower. And by such disorder it commeth to pass that the most vertuous are despised, whilest the naughtie – packes and vicious fellowes are esteemed and made much of.
>
> (Beard 1631: 3)

In Beard's opinion, men restrained from sin as much by their own understanding as by Grace have a natural perception of value:

> Now to the end that no man should pretend ignorance for an excuse God hath bestowed on everie one a certaine knowledge and judgment of good and evill: which being naturally engraven in the tables of man's hearts, is commonly called the Law of Nature.
>
> (Beard 1631: V, 9)

The laws which govern society are therefore perceptible both to man and to God, who agree on priorities:

the law of God and man is termed all that which God and man allow and agree upon, and which a man with safe conscience may put into practice.

(Beard 1631: XIX, 448)

The overwhelming factor of Beard's presentation of faith is its immediate active dimension. Respect for God's will implies an understanding of good and evil, and a readiness and an ability to act on this knowledge. The importance of these qualities in a social context is recurrently stressed by Beard. He points out the seriousness of a deliberate refusal on the part of those in power to respect the law agreed on by God and man. He says that such men

do boldly exempt themselves from all corrections and punishments due unto them, being altogether unwilling to be subject to any order of justice or law whatsoever . . .

(Beard 1631: I, 7)

At the point where restraints imposed by human agencies have no effect, Beard states, God takes over and 'himself becometh executioner of his own justice upon their paths'. God is seen as a more efficient magistrate than a man, but as intent on fitting the punishment to the crime as the godly citizen. Beard points out that God has a sense of fairness with regard to man's social position. It is easy to see when God's justice is at work, rather than mere misfortune:

If any man of low degree meet with adversity, people say he was destitute of help. But if a great man is overtaken or surprised by any great evil . . . in this we must acknowledge the hand of God.

(Beard 1631: I, 8)

Beard's emphasis is repeatedly on the misuse of power. He points out the danger of power combined with arrogance, and warns against a complacency of this kind; through it, we break the commandment to love God above all else:

it is . . . a breach of the first commandment . . . when we ascribe not to God the glorie of his benefits to give him thanks for them, but through a foolish pride extoll ourselves higher than we ought presuming above measured reason in our own power, desire to place ourselves in a higher degree than is meet.

(Beard 1631: XXII, 127)

Quite clearly, 'measured reason' has an important part to play in reminding men of appropriate behaviour, and in warning them to draw limits to their claims. Beard stresses the wrong of going to war for the purpose of indulging human power:

> As in surgerie, so in a commonwealth, wee must account warre as a last refuge, which without verie urgent necessitie, when all other meanes of maintaining our estate against the assults of the enemie . . . ought not to be taken in hand.
>
> (Beard 1631: XXII, 344)

The differences between Calvin and Beard are illuminating. Calvin's stress on interiority is again the most important disparity in their focus. In contrast with Calvin's insistence on man's need to develop his awareness of the distance between him and God, Beard indicates the potential in man to achieve, through his understanding of God's will, 'a conversation with life'. Whereas Calvin points to the Bible almost exclusively as the source of knowledge of God's will, Beard insists equally on the revelation afforded by contemporary events. The salient point of Beard's understanding of God's will is that it offers man an immediate moral directive, thus enabling him to play a fairer role in society. When Beard warns against presuming 'above measured reason', he is already giving 'measured reason' a certain validity. His definition of sin refers to man's ability to avoid sin:

> there is not a man living, which doth not know in his own heart, that he doeth an evil deed when he wrongeth another.
>
> (Beard 1631: V, 9)

This is directive from experience, from the heart, from the conscience. However, combined with a confidence in man's natural ability to act on the good, there remains in Beard's outlook a fundamental humility which derives from Calvin's suspicion of the human condition, a humility which demands deference to God's will, and a consciousness of its overwhelming importance, and which totally supersedes the self-interest of any individual. In this way, many later Calvinists developed the conviction that a vocation called them to action in accordance with God's plan.

It is possible to identify in Oliver Cromwell's responses to the situations in which he found himself a moral perspective which owed much to this outlook. The climate of the times in which he lived certainly encouraged Cromwell to respond to the call of events. The age was saturated with providentialism. Cromwell's letters of the early 1640s abound with testimonies to the power of God who, he claims, was exclusively responsible for the victories of the parliamentary army. Writing to his brother-in-law after the battle of Marston Moor, Cromwell states of the opposing army: 'God made them stubble to our swords' (Abbott: I, 287).

Similarly his account of the taking of a house in Bletchindon in April 1645 demonstrates his appreciation of God's intervention:

> This was the mercy of God, and nothing is more due than a real acknowledgement. And though I have had greater mercies, yet none clearer: because, in the first place God brought them into our hands when we had not looked for them; and delivered them out of our hands, when we had laid a reasonable design to surprise them, which we carefully endeavoured. His mercy appears in this also, that I did much doubt the storming of the house, it being strong and well manned and I having few dragoons . . . and yet we got it.
>
> (Abbott: I, 287)

Cromwell saw hope for their campaign in God's assistance alone, and implored his followers not to place their confidence in their own efforts:

> I hope you will pardon me if I say God is not enough owned. We look too much to men and visible helps: this has much hindered our success. But I hope God will direct all to acknowledge Him alone in all things.
>
> (Abbott: I, 340)

Cromwell's account of his own state of mind before the battle of Naseby provides a good description of the relaxed confidence which he thought must inevitably ensue if faith in God were complete: because he was so sure that their cause was God's cause, he trusted God to give his soldiers victory irrespective of their material resources:

> I could not (riding about my own business) but smile in praises to God in assurance of victory, because God would, by all things which are not, bring to naught things that are. Of which I had great assurance, and God did it.
>
> (Abbott: I, 365)

This attitude is clearly more complex than the aphorism 'Trust in

God and keep your powder dry', by which Cromwell is most widely known. In Cromwell's view, shown in the above observations, the human ability to keep the powder dry was nothing to be relied on, and to trust in God was no easy task: it was a great spiritual challenge, demanding the extension of the mind beyond its natural limits, endeavouring to identify the will of God before the intentions of man. Cromwell's letter to the Speaker of the House of Commons recounting the capture of Bristol gives an idea of the readiness of his soldiers to be directed by God's will. He claims that they fully understood the true nature of the power behind their victory:

> It's their joy that they are instruments to God's glory and their country's good; it's their honour that God vouchsafes to use them. Sir, they that have been employed in this service know that faith and prayer obtained this city for you. I do not say ours only, but of the people of God with you and all England over, who have wrestled with God for a blessing in this very thing.
>
> (Abbott: I, 377)

To Cromwell, the parliamentary cause was the cause of God and it therefore lay far from human self-interest. One day, he trusted, God would make this clear. In 1644, he wrote to Colonel Walton:

> God . . . will in due time, make it appear to the world that we study the glory of God and the honor and liberty of our parliament, for which we unanimously fight, without seeking our own interests.
>
> (Abbott: I, 292)

He adds in this letter that he would never have been able to satisfy himself on 'the justness of this war', but for the authority of the parliament to maintain itself and its right:

> And in this cause I hope to approve myself an honest man and single hearted.
>
> (Abbott: I, 292)

The series of events which delivered Charles I into the hands of the Parliamentarian army were, to Cromwell, the supreme example of the working of God's will. In a letter to his brother-in-law, Col. Robert Hammond, coincidentally in command of the Isle of Wight when Charles fled there, Cromwell laid great emphasis on the mystery behind this extraordinary series of events.

If thou wilt seek to know the mind of God in all that chain of Providence wherby God brought thee hither and that person [i.e. Charles I] to thee; how before and since, God has ordered him and affairs concerning him; and then tell me whether there be not some glorious and high meaning in all this, above what thou has yet attained? And, laying aside thy fleshly reason, seek of the Lord to teach thee what that is; and he will do it.

(Abbott: I, 696)

The effect of Providentialism and the second generation of Calvinists in England might appear to be an unjustified amplification of a particular situation or a personal circumstance. However, it is important to bear in mind the recurrent contrast Cromwell makes in his letters between the acting out of God's will, and what he saw as his own insignificant identity. His own actions and God's will are not equal in his eyes, although he hoped that the former would be directed by the latter. His hope for himself is that he might prove to be 'an honest man and single hearted'. This kind of honesty and integrity could only be derived, in his view, as in that of Thomas Beard, by a repression of his own interests and of any sense of self-importance. In this way, the original polarities established by Calvin between the supremacy of God's will and the relative insignificance of the individual man are sustained.

Throughout his time of command of the army and of power in parliament, Cromwell was conscious of the need to subdue any appetite for personal power that might overtake him.

His speech to the Speaker of the House of Commons on 9 December 1644 makes it clear that he did not call on his soldiers for exclusive loyalty to his command. The Speaker, who symbolized the rights of parliament, was the focus of their allegiance:

I can speak this for my own soldiers that they look not upon me, but upon you; and for you they will fight and live and die in your cause; and if others be of that mind that they are of, you need not fear them. They do not idolize me, but look upon the cause they fight for.

(Abbott: I, 316)

All his life, Cromwell endeavoured to balance the favour that he thought God had shown him with a sense of the value of others. His readiness to listen to another's point of view has often been seen as hypocrisy (see Morrill 1990: 206), but when seen in the light of Beard's moral criteria, its cause becomes clear: power was dangerous because it could lead to an illusion of self-importance. Cromwell kept a sense of humility; he listened to others and was absorbent. He sought the unity of the godly, but not for political reasons. Some attitudes he refused to ally himself with, notably those which sought the exclusion of others and claimed a privileged authority. Just as he was determined not to impose human authority between grace and the soul, he would not allow others to attempt to do this either. His opposition to Presbyterianism was for this reason as adamant as his opposition to Roman Catholicism, and his later suspicion of 'licentious' sects.

In his declaration of the English army when they marched on Scotland, he stated that the march was undertaken 'to defend liberty of conscience against a nation bent on defying providence to coerce consciences'. He claimed that 'God would work what He willed in the minds of men' (Abbott: II, 285–6). Cromwell's aim has been described as to formulate 'policies designed to prevent the godly from disturbing one another in their pursuit of godliness' (Morrill 1990: 193).

Cromwell's self-appointed role as constable appears unambitious, or otherwise designed as a camouflage. However, its priority would appear to have been an intention to avoid self-assertion. His whole period of office is notable for its absence of policy. In the words of J.C. Davis:

> The Cromwellian regime has frequently been criticized for an absence of clear policy objectives and of management strategies for their realization. But such criticism overlooks the fact that reliance on providence implied in one sense, the absence of policy, the forgoing of trust in fleshly reasoning and its instruments and institutions.
>
> (Morrill 1990: 187)

Cromwell's suspicion of man-made institutions led to the most radical element of his thought although, paradoxically, it prevented him from allying himself ultimately with the most radical thinkers of his time. His suspicion of all human interpretation constituted a fundamental challenge, potentially as erosive as Jansenism would be in France in the 1660s. His tolerance derived from his suspicion of his own spiritual authority, but it did not allow him to commit himself to any particular partisan line. He was sceptical about any human claim to know the right way, but had a sense of

'the unfathomable nature of providence in its choice of instrument':
this led to a kind of *laissez-faire* approach to the doings of God.

Cromwell's reluctance to exert an exclusive authority did not
mean that his attitude was passive. Of some things he was certain,
and of these, the essential was the inadequacy of man-made moral
categories. The New Model Army was made up of men 'who had
the root of the matter in them'. In 1645, he wrote to the Speaker of
the House of Commons:

> Presbyterians, Independents, all had here the same spirit of faith
> and prayer: pity is it should be otherwise anywhere. All that
> believe have the real unity, which is most glorious, because
> inward and spiritual, in the Body and the Head. As for being
> united in forms . . . every Christian will for peaces sake study
> and do, as far as conscience will permit; and from brethren, in
> things of the mind we look for no compulsion, but that of light
> and reason.
>
> (Abbott: I, 377)

This Miltonic phrase suggests a confidence in the human ability to
have a 'conversation with life', understanding in terms beyond
self-interest, prompted by the conscience and respect for the freedom of the other. This spirit, he was to hope all his life, would
transcend the squabbling of sects. Together with his rejection of the
validity of divisions of religious practices, Cromwell also rejected
the notion of inbuilt class superiority: his comments to a friend in
Cambridge about the worth of the officers in his army make this
clear:

> I had rather have a plain russet-coated captain that knows what
> he fights for, and loves what he knows, than that which you call
> a gentleman and nothing else.
>
> (Abbott: I, 377)

In Cromwell's private life, he appeared determined to make his
respect of others' consciences known. It is interesting that he kept
a Quaker servant. At the other extreme, he apparently protested at
the execution of a Jesuit in 1654, claiming to be vigorously opposed
to violence in matters of religion (see Morrill 1990: 197). The Instrument of Government, however, offered toleration 'to all but Roman
Catholics and the licentious'.

It was possibly one of the fundamental frustrations of Cromwell's position as Protector that it was impossible to pass laws

which had the spiritual dimensions of Christian values. For this reason, one may not look to his legislation for an indication of how he intended to implement moral priorities. Perhaps the closest of any of his political moves towards this was the establishment of the Nominated Assembly of 1653, which was to consist of men drawn from the 'several sorts of Godliness in the nation'. Notably he refused to sit on it himself. This idea was far from a Machiavellian device to put in power people who would agree with him; far from enslaving men, it was meant to offer a lesson in spiritual responsibility. As John Morrill has said:

> Cromwell could only seek to create transitional structures that could help the people learn their duty of obedience to the will of God.
>
> (Morrill 1990: 14)

Cromwell's refusal to accept the crown again stemmed from a motive of self-effacement. As well as seeking freedom for his fellow godly citizens to act according to their consciences, he sought this freedom himself.

The stress on the sensitivity of Cromwell's conscience might, in some ways, appear inappropriate. From 1647 onwards former friends thought he had betrayed them; the Levellers decided that his campaign for civil rights was exclusively a quest for personal power. His elimination of the radical element in the army at Burford Bridge was to many a treacherous act. It became clear, to thinkers like Gerard Winstanley, that Cromwell's parliament was unlikely to establish the rule of the country along egalitarian lines.

However, Cromwell was intrinsically conservative; he believed that the godly order would emerge from within the context of the existing social order. The essential challenge as Cromwell saw it was to provide for a change in the hearts and minds, the beliefs and actions of individuals. Cromwell thought that restrictions must be imposed on any that sought to challenge the principles of behaviour laid down in the Gospel:

> As for the profane persons, blasphemers, such as preach sedition, the contentious railers, evil speakers who seek by evil words to corrupt good manners, persons of loose conversation, punishment from the civil magistrate ought to meet with them, because if they plead conscience, yet walking disorderly, and

not according but contrary to the Gospel and even natural light,
they are judges all . . .

(Abbott: III, 585–6)

Cromwell's mentality was not democratic. He insisted on tolerance, but this did not mean that he was willing to concede validity
to any human interpretation of things, and certainly he would deny
any validity at all to attitudes or behaviours that flouted the Gospel.
His aim was unity, but this did not indicate any idea that there
might be an accordance of views; he hoped more for an admission
of the intrinsic fallibility of any view devised in human self-interest,
and not subservient to the will of God. His plea to the Scottish Kirk
before the battle of Dunbar defines the responsibility Cromwell
thought all men should accept:

> I beseech you in the bowels of Christ, think it possible you may
> be mistaken.

(Abbott: II, 303)

A few days after the battle, his defence of the liberty of conscience
to the governor of Edinburgh castle suggests the positive side of
Cromwell's outlook:

> It will be found an unjust and unwise jealousy to deny a man
> the liberty he hath by nature upon a supposition he may abuse
> it. When he doth abuse it, judge.

(Abbott: II, 338)

This built-in reservation about denying natural liberty clearly had
its boundary. The modern reader thinks inevitably of Drogheda.
Although the massacre perpetrated by Cromwell's troops both
here and at Wexford seems unwarranted and inhumane, it is
important to remember that Cromwell embarked on the campaign
in Ireland with an order forbidding plunder and pillage. In the case
of Drogheda, when it became clear that any defence the inhabitants
might offer would henceforth be to no avail, Cromwell summoned
them and warned them of the consequences of a refusal to capitu-
late. What followed was in accordance with the contemporary rules
of warfare. The only positive factor Cromwell could see in this
event was that this 'bitterness' would act as a deterrent to any
future resistance. Furthermore, Cromwell genuinely believed that
he was bringing freedom to the hapless Irish, who were generally
regarded as culturally inferior to the English, and therefore in need

of stewardship to find any sense of moral direction. Cromwell made a point of denying that the only reason for establishing power in Ireland was to make it impossible for Charles Stuart to invade England from there. He declared on his campaign:

> We come (by the assistance of God) to hold forth and maintain the lustre and glory of English liberty in a nation where we have an undoubted right to do it; wherein the people of Ireland . . . may equally participate in all benefits, to use liberty and fortune equally with Englishmen, if they keep out of arms.
>
> (Hill 1973: 115)

It is clear that Cromwell was thinking, even in his attempt to pacify Ireland, of securing the liberty of the Irish, not their enslavement.

It is perhaps surprising that, in the course of such extreme social upheaval, it is possible to distinguish a moral profile of Cromwell. Had his behaviour been exclusively pragmatic, as some have claimed, such an attempt would be doomed, since there would be as little consistency to his responses as there was in the extreme and unprecedented events that befell him. In fact, the priorities defined by Beard would seem to make an independent sense of Cromwell's reactions. Cromwell's period of power was tempered by his suspicion of power.

His great fear was of misreading the will of God; his consistent personal effort was to acquire a humility which would ensure his deference to it.

In the February before he died, Cromwell wrote:

> I would have been glad, as to my own conscience and spirit, to have been living under a woodside, to have kept a flock of sheep, rather than to have undertaken such a place as this was.
>
> (Abbott: IV, 729)

Such a humble calling, Cromwell implies, would have been more comprehensible to him. However, his very diffidence about his own abilities was his saving grace; in his own words, 'a man never rises higher than when he knows not where he is going' (Hill 1973: 188).

Chapter 5

Winstanley: the values of experience

During the 1640s, when the parliamentary army was offering a radical challenge to the assumptions of local aristocrats, the whole of England was in a state of ferment. The army's action stirred people all over the country to question an acquiescence they had hitherto taken for granted. Parliament's need for support amongst the masses led it to permit a climate of toleration in which discussion of religious and spiritual matters could take place, unsupervised and uncensored, throughout the community. It was in such a climate that Gerrard Winstanley began to think and to write.

Winstanley was born in 1609 in Wigan, the son of a middle-class Puritan family. He was apprenticed to a clothier, married and set up business just before the outbreak of civil war severed connections between Lancashire and London, where he now lived (see Hill 1990: 114). His business was ruined as a consequence. He became a hired labourer in Surrey, where he looked after cows. He suffered great poverty, as did very many people towards the end of the decade. Not only was there devastation as a result of the civil wars, but bad harvest led to famine and disease. The execution of Charles I prompted the appearance of pamphlets advocating the use of confiscated church property to provide for the poor: a millenarian feeling prevailed amongst many people.

Winstanley's ideas emanate from the heady climate of these times: this is clear from their intensity, and the impression they give of a sense of spiritual directive. Their interest lies in their apparent independence of external organization. Whereas Cromwell awaited the falling out of events to show him how to act, Winstanley's thinking transcended immediate event and created its own universe. The source of his perspective was essentially interior, and the values which this inner experience showed him were the criteria of his faith.

Winstanley was initially a Puritan church-goer 'believing as the learned clergy believed' (Winstanley 1941: 243). Subsequently, he became a Baptist, but went further still from any organized way of thinking about religion. In one of his earliest pamphlets, *Truth Lifting up its Head*, which he wrote in 1648, he says:

> I see now that it is not the material water, but the water of life; that is the spirit, in which soules are to be dipped, and so drawn out into the one spirit, and all these outward customes and formes are to cease and pass away.
>
> (Winstanley 1941: 141)

His understanding of the nature of faith led him to reject 'outward customes and formes'. His greatest conviction of truth came to him while he was quiet at his work. He expresses it in terms of a personal revelation: 'my heart was filled with sweet thoughts, and many things were revealed to me which I had never read in books, nor heard from the mouth of any flesh' (Winstanley 1973: 127). He claimed to have heard the words 'Work together, break bread together', and, to show his readiness to obey this command, he took his spade to 'break the ground on George Hill'. To Winstanley, this was a symbolic act, he was:

> thereby declaring freedom to the creation, and that the earth must be set free from entanglements of lords and landlords and that it shall become a common treasury to all, as it was first made and given to the sons of men.
>
> (Winstanley 1973: 128)

In the economic crisis of 1649, when there was starvation in London, mutiny in the New Model Army, and a general impatience to see the introduction of fairer distribution, Winstanley decided that the time had come to make a symbolic declaration of his ownership of the land, which he did together with a group of poor men.

This action hardly constituted a grave threat to the property owners of England, but local landlords became alarmed. Two of the principal Diggers, Everard and Winstanley, were brought before General Fairfax. They told him that they hoped all the poor would soon do as they had done, and that property owners would voluntarily abandon their estates and involve themselves in communal production. Fairfax genially concluded that they were mad, and dismissed the anxiety of local landowners. The latter then took things into their own hands, and raided and destroyed the houses and crops on George Hill. By the winter of 1649, the Digger colony was virtually annihilated.

Winstanley saw his action as symbolic, and it is in this way that it must be understood. What did it symbolize? To answer this, it must be placed in the context of Winstanley's thinking. We have seen how he refused to acknowledge any precedent for his 'sweet thoughts'. In the first Digger manifesto, *The True Levellers' Standard Advanced*, Winstanley asserts the importance of judging by standards of which one is oneself aware (Winstanley 1973). Men should reject 'outward teachers', he declares. Winstanley identifies the ability of man to think and judge as the Spirit of the Creator. Man can find this Spirit within himself. It is wrong to suppress this ability, and to submit to the teaching of others, for this might well undermine one's perception: 'every single man, male and female, is a perfect creature of himself: and the same spirit that made the globe dwells in man to govern the globe' (Winstanley 1973: 77).

Until now, spurious authorities have claimed to have access to all truth, denying the validity of the experience of poor people: 'the secrets of creation have been locked up under the traditional parrot-like speaking from the universities' (Winstanley 1973: 109). He calls the great creator Reason, and claims that it is man's ability to reason that tells him his creator is within him. For Winstanley, reason is not speculative or erudite; it is a definitive quality in itself, very much as Descartes saw it. Reason is common sense, which every individual establishes through reference to his own judgement. Winstanley's confidence in the ability of all men to make valid judgements gave him the ability to identify fully with others. Far from setting himself up as a leader with unique authority, he was convinced that the truth as he saw it was available to anyone, if they allowed themselves to see it.

Winstanley's assertion of the intrinsic value of the human spirit was not, however, a glorification of man in his present condition. He claimed that men had allowed the spirit of peace and liberty to be quashed or dammed up by the teaching power of the self-interested, and by the intrusion of covetousness. Winstanley not only located the spirit of reason in man, but identified sin in him also. However, this was not the crippling, original sin which Calvin saw as blighting every human endeavour. Winstanley saw what was wrong in the human condition as man's responsibility; just as he had caused it, he could change it. By allowing himself to be crushed, man had compromised his perfection. Winstanley interprets this process in a surprisingly modern way, while drawing on Biblical allegory. The beginnings of man's enslavement to covetousness began, asserts Winstanley, when he started to 'delight in the objects of creation, more than in the spirit of reason and righteousness' (Winstanley 1973: 77). This covetousness led to a 'blindness of mind and weakness of heart' and caused men to abdicate their power of judgement, submitting to other external forces. Winstanley regards *imagination* as a subversive ingredient in the human make-up. It was as devastating a force in Winstanley's mind as it was in that of Pascal, the Jansenist writer (Pascal 1960: 81,125). Winstanley understands imagination as the misleading force that distorts true judgement, and prevents men from conceiving values clearly. In his pamphlet *Fire in the Bush* he writes:

> When mankind is guided by imagination, he runs a great hazard upon life and death. This power is he that calls good evil and evil good, this knows not the creating spirit in inward feeling, but does fancy himself to be sometimes one thing, sometimes another; and still dwells in the dark chamber of uncertainty.
>
> (Winstanley 1973: 22)

Imagination exchanges a clear understanding of what *is* for an illusion of the possibility of self-indulgence and luxury. It leads men to 'lust after everything they see or hear of'. Even if they acquire what they imagine to be their desire, they are still troubled by doubts and uncertainties. When they find themselves disappointed and deceived, they see themselves 'naked and ashamed', Winstanley says. In his pamphlet *Fire in the Bush* Winstanley allegorizes the story of the garden of Eden and presents imagination as the lure of the tree of knowledge, describing it as the source of man's destruction: 'selfish, unwarranted and unexperienced imagination' is man's 'sickness and disease' and leads him to lose his honour and his strength. Essentially, imagination thrives on fiction perpetuated by the deceived.

Winstanley sees the power of imagination as holding sway in his own times; he diagnoses the sickness of his age thus:

> the whole world of mankind generally at this day, through all the nations of the world, is eating out of this tree of knowledge

of good and evil and are cast out of themselves, and know not
the power that rules in them: and so are ignorant of their God.
(Winstanley 1973: 221)

It is clear that Winstanley sees it possible to find a remedy for the
debilitating effects of this self-induced malady; through reverting
to his own authentic judgement, man can dispel the poison spread
by the lure of covetousness and of imaginary possessions. In his
interpretation of the ills of his time, Winstanley is updating the
myth of the Everlasting Gospel, a doctrine widespread in Europe
by the 1640s and which had been taken over by the Familists (see
Hill 1975: 147). This myth divided human history into three ages:
the Age of Law, the Age of the Gospel and the Age of the Spirit.
The third age, it was believed by contemporary radical movements,
was the present, when men were in the process of being delivered
from all forms and ordinances. Winstanley characterizes this third
age as the time at which men would reject imaginary and hearsay
doctrines to assert the values of reason, experience and universal
love. He understood his own perceptions to imply that this age had
come. He did not see himself as a Messiah, but he thought that his
readiness to speak and act on the truth, as he saw it, was part of a
great movement in which many would do the same.

Like that of the other Diggers, Winstanley's experience was that
land was wrongly distributed; the Diggers claimed that the people
had been robbed of and deluded about their rightful inheritance of
the earth. The opening sentence of his pamphlet *A True Levellers'
Standard Advanced* declares the earth a 'common treasury'. Covetousness and imagination had warped men's minds, so that they
submitted to a system which sets one man over another. The earth
was no longer seen as a common heritage, but was bought and sold.
Therefore, men had received a false idea of their creator. He was
wrongly presented as a 'respector of persons, delighting in the
comfortable livelihood of some, and rejoicing in the miserable
poverty and straits of others' (Winstanley 1973: 78). Men had
brought this evil on themselves, not only by submitting to covetousness, but by acquiescing before that of others. They had
allowed their hearts to be filled with 'slavish fears of others' and
had 'looked abroad' for righteousness, rather than within themselves. It was a kind of *mauvaise foi*, to use a twentieth-century
existentialist term, whereby man denies his own freedom.

This fallen state, then, was no more than a misguided complicity with exploitation. Winstanley regarded his own ability to identify such evil forces as an element of the capacity for regeneration within man. Calvin had said that if a man wished to find the devil, he need look no further than himself. Winstanley would add to this that, if a man wished to find Christ, he need look no further than himself either. Christ's coming was what another radical, Samuel Fish, described as 'his coming into man by his spirit'. Winstanley said that he lived in 'a time of the son of man . . . when man could speak, like a child rising upward towards manhood' (Winstanley 1973: 81). The ways in which the common people were becoming aware of the oppression under which they laboured indicated that deliverance was at hand:

> the spirit of Christ, which is the spirit of universal community and freedom, is risen and is rising, and will rise higher and higher, till those pure waters of Shiloah, the well springs of life and liberty to the whole creation, do overrun A-Dam and drown those banks of bondage, curse and slavery.
> (Winstanley 1973: 88)

Winstanley claimed to be giving voice in his pamphlets to the people's rejection of the government under which they then lived. In his pamphlet *Declaration from the Poor Oppressed People of England*, he makes the following statement to the wealthy: 'seeing and finding ourselves poor, and wanting food to feed upon while we labour the earth we are willing to declare our condition to you and all that have the treasury of the earth locked up in your bags, chests and barns'. In the pamphlet he arraigns the economic evil which is at the root of their oppression: 'buying and selling is the great cheat that robs and steals the earth one from another' (Winstanley 1973: 101, 102). His target here is the government established by Cromwell since the parliamentarian victory, and particularly the survival of the old laws protecting ownership of the land. He sees this as an appropriation of common resources, dating back to the Norman Invasion. The victories of Cromwell's army had done nothing to divide the land fairly. Cromwell's government refused to admit the part played by the people in the defeat of the Royalists – as great a part, claims Winstanley, as that played by the old lords of the manor:

> if the lords of manors lay claim to the earth over us from the Army's victories over the king, then we have as much right to

the land as they, because our labours and blood and death of friends were the purchasers of the earth's freedom as well as theirs.

(Winstanley 1973: 282)

Winstanley's confidence in the perspective from which he saw life inspired in him a trenchant criticism of what he identified as unfair, hypocritical attitudes. He tells Oliver Cromwell how the people remembered his promises of liberty, whereas now, after his victory, 'inferior, common people can hardly keep a cow, but half starve her. . . . Country people cannot sell any corn or fruits of the earth in a market town, but they must either pay toll or be turned out of the town' (Winstanley 1973: 281). Oliver has done nothing to change the laws, which still restrict the people, and are a shackling irrelevancy to their lives: '[laws] are but the cords, bonds, manacles and yokes that the enslaved English like Newgate prisoners wear upon their hands and legs as they walk the streets' (Winstanley 1973: 86). The people live under 'confusion and blindness' since they have been deceived by 'plausible words of flattery'.

Such challenges read like political invective, designed to have a stirring rhetorical effect. Yet Winstanley was supremely conscious of a dimension beyond analysis and arraignment: 'thoughts run in me that words and writing were all nothing and must die, for action is the life of all, and if thou dost not act, thou dost nothing' (Winstanley 1973: 127). His call to action was, however, not militant. Violent uprising was not, for him, the legitimate means of assisting the coming of Christ's kingdom:

we shall meddle with none of your properties . . . till the spirit in you make you cast up your lands and goods . . . and then we shall take it from the spirit that has conquered you, and not from our swords, which is an abominable and unrighteous power and a destroyer of the creation . . . the son came not to destroy but to save.

(Winstanley 1973: 103)

He looked upon the owners of the land as their own worst enemies; his aim was not to conquer them but to enlighten them. The action to which Winstanley called his fellows was to 'work together, obeying the lord of hosts'. He called upon the parliament and the army to 'join in this work and find peace'. This work was not metaphorical; indeed, it was described succinctly in his pamphlet addressed to the City of London and the army as the act of digging up, manuring and sowing corn on the common land. He described the community of Diggers as essentially loving people: 'We have ploughed and digged upon George Hill in Surrey to sow corn for the succour of man offering no offence to any, but do carry ourselves in love and peace towards all' (Winstanley 1973: 112). Winstanley claimed to have found in the Digger community a way of acting and living which approximated to his faith. Manuring the soil was a religious act, he said. The community was a microcosm of God's will:

> all the prophecies on the Scriptures and reason are encircled here within this community, and mankind must have the law of righteousness once more writ in his heart, and all must be of one heart and one mind.
>
> (Winstanley 1973: 80)

If this happens, he claims, all enmity will cease. The blessing of deliverance was to spring from the poor common people who work and break bread together: they 'lift up creation from bondage'.

Winstanley understood his position on many levels. He allegorized the Bible, presenting sin as the wilful enslavement of man to the power of the imaginary lure. He presented resurrection and salvation as the flooding into man of love and essential reason. It was sinful to collude with those who defended private property and the exploitation of their fellows. It was doing good to nurture the common land. Put in these terms, Winstanley's argument appears theoretical – at best, theological. But, as he himself said, words have no power; power lies in action alone. Compared with the action of Cromwell's New Model Army, Winstanley's action might appear little short of pathetic. However, his experience of digging on George Hill with his fellows, and the aggressive abuse this aroused, was an encounter between two incompatible forces, which reveals much about the essential moral identity of each. In the document addressed to the court in Kingston, where Winstanley presented the case of the Diggers, the moral strength of his outlook is overwhelming. In simple terms, which refer to no political or religious concepts to fill them out, without rhetorical development to reinforce their impact, he describes his reaction to the assault on his home and goods. His account is of the immediate moment, yet at the same time an expression of his readiness to accept that he cannot understand everything:

if I could not get meat to eat, I would feed upon bread and milk and cheese; and if they take the cows, that I cannot feed on this or hereby make a breach between me and them that owns the cows, then I'll feed upon bread and beer till the king of righteousness doth come and clear upon my innocence and the justice of his own cause; and if this be taken from me for maintaining this cause, I'll stand still and see what he will do with me for as yet I know not.

(Winstanley 1973: 139)

His cows were indeed taken away, and beaten and clubbed, 'and yet [he writes] these cows were never upon George Hill nor digged upon the ground, and yet the poor beasts must suffer because they gave milk to me' (Winstanley 1973: 141). He is aware that he has no physical power to drive away his aggressors. But he is conscious of a spiritual victory:

though you should kill my body or starve me in a prison, yet know that the more you strive, the more troubles your heart shall be filled with; and do the worst you can to hinder public freedom, you shall come off losers in the latter end, I mean you shall lose your kingdom of darkness, though I lose my livelihood, the poor cows that is my living.

(Winstanley 1973: 144)

From an objective point of view, Winstanley's position appears untenable. But his confidence in his own judgement and his faith in a fundamental order beyond himself yet of which he is part, enable him to be indifferent to external criteria:

I see, Father, that England yet does choose to fight with the sword of iron and covetousness than by the sword of thy spirit (which is love); and what thy purpose is with this land or with my body I know not; but establish thy power within me and do what pleaseth thee.

(Winstanley 1973: 140)

He felt, he says, like a man in a storm standing under a shelter upon a hill, in peace.

Winstanley's interiority is a dimension in his life that has been largely neglected. Yet in terms of his moral evaluation he achieved something rare: he was able to identify the values of his creator as those operating within his own mind. His experience of his faith is the experience of his life: he refuses to be mystified. The realities of his life are the terms of his dialogue with God; he needs no language other than this.

The degree to which Winstanley established spiritual independence of all but the insights of his own experience brings to mind the outlook of Michel de Montaigne. Although Montaigne was writing at the end of the sixteenth century in France, there were similarities between that climate and the one in which Winstanley wrote. The country had been decimated by civil war, doctrines had been proclaimed as absolute, and both Winstanley and Montaigne turned to their own judgement to establish more valid criteria.

It may at first appear odd to bring together Montaigne, an intellectual French recluse of the late sixteenth century, with an Englishman of the following century so involved in what might be termed political activity. Yet there are striking similarities between them. Montaigne's decision to withdraw from his office of Mayor of Bordeaux was a consequence of his dissatisfaction with the public life of his time. 'Montaigne et le Maire sont deux', he pronounced. He had a great respect for Machiavelli, whose conclusion that moral integrity and power were incompatible he echoes. The only area in which Montaigne saw a possibility of establishing a valid moral perspective was within the confines of his own life. His original intention was to build up his moral resources through reading and writing, inspired by the Stoic death of his friend Etienne de la Boetie. However, from the beginning he was suspicious of a purely intellectual approach and turned to his experience to be the arbiter of values.

Montaigne's increasing scepticism was the basis of his assessment of intellectual assertions. In the *Apologie de Raymond Sebond* he reaches the apogee of his rejection of human pretentiousness. Like Winstanley, he contests the intrinsic validity of man-made laws; it is only men's readiness to submit to them that gives them their authority:

Les loix prennent leur authorité de la possession et de l'usage

The authority of the laws lies in the fact that men possess them and use them

(Montaigne 1962: II.XII.257)

Montaigne shares with Winstanley an appreciation of the willingness of people to be mystified; ceremony and pomp, he wrote, do much to convince. The respect shown to people in high office comes from a kind of social superstition. The power of laws is a mystique:

> les loix se maintiennent en credit non par ce qu'elle sont justes, mais par ce qu'elles sont loix. C'est le fondement mystique de leur authorité; elles n'en ont point d'autre

> laws retain their credit not because they are just but because they are laws. This is the mystical foundation of their authority; they have no other
>
> Montaigne 1962: III.XIII.1,049)

In the *Apologie*, Montaigne challenges human pretentiousness, insisting on the essential limitations of man's condition, and the inevitable inadequacy of perception. Man's knowledge is no sure foundation, and gives no insight into essential truth:

> Car tout philosophe ignore ce que faict son voisin, ouy et ce qu'il fait luy-mesme, et ignore ce qu'ils sont tous deux . . .

> For no philosopher knows what his neighbour is doing, nor what he is doing himself, and knows not what either of them is . . .
>
> (Montaigne 1962: II.XII.520)

Montaigne's scepticism, however, is not totally negative. It has the effect of making him suspicious of all systemetized knowledge and claims to authority. His rejection of intellectual wisdom brings him very close to Winstanley's scorn of 'parrot-like universities' and he asserts the value of the Socratic precept of an awareness of one's own ignorance. But Montaigne is conscious of criteria which do make for valid judgements. He contrasts what he considers to be the pretentious remedies supplied by physicians with the instinctive response to sickness of a field labourer:

> Compares la vie d'un homme asservy a telles imaginations a celle d'un laboureur se laissant aller apres son appetit naturel, mesurant les choses au seul sentiment present, sans science et sans prognostique, qui n'a du mal que lorsqu'il l'a . . .

> Compare the life of a man befuddled with such delusions with that of a field labourer, allowing himself to follow his natural appetite, judging things only by what he currently feels, without knowledge nor prognosis, who only has pain when he feels it . . .
>
> (Montaigne 1962: II.XII.470)

It is interesting that Montaigne uses the term 'imaginations' to describe the delusions of the spurious medical practitioners: he anticipates Pascal in his consciousness of man's capacity for self-delusion and, like Winstanley, sees false perception as undermining valid understanding. It is interesting too that Montaigne takes his example of straightforward response from the poor people; again, like Winstanley, he saw the supposedly superior knowledge of the educated class as a hindrance rather than a source of enlightenment.

He rejected criteria established by pretentious authorities and also by opinion. He insisted that values should not be derived from external impressions; it is an inner knowledge of ourselves which alone can decide on our worth:

> Ce n'est pas pour la montre que nostre ame doit jouer son rolle, c'est chez nous au dedans, d'ou nuls yeux ne donnent que les nostres . . .

> It is not for show that our soul must play its part, it is for ourselves alone, where no eyes may see but ours . . .
> (Montaigne 1962: II.XVI.607)

This emphasis on inner contentment and rejection of the opinion of the world again has affinities with the attitude Winstanley will adopt to his persecutors on George Hill, when he is happy to stand as if sheltering from a storm under a tree, at peace. Both Winstanley and Montaigne found within themselves an inner strength which compensated for the inadequacy and mistaken assumptions of the judgements they observed in the society around them.

Montaigne is well known for his decision to move away from presenting a generalized observation of humanity in his essays and instead to concentrate on the particular: himself. He finds that within his own experience he can find the wisdom he needs to enable him to understand the terms of his existence:

> De l'experience que j'ay de moy, je trouve assez dequoy me faire sage si j'estoy bon escholier . . .

> From the experience which I have of myself, I find enough to make me wise, if I am diligent enough in my studies . . .
> (Montaigne 1962: III.XIII.1,051)

It is of course a mistake to assume that, in recounting life from the perspective of his own experience, Montaigne dismisses any truth beyond the immediate. Montaigne's apprehension of a meta-physical absolute was sufficient to allow him an ability to appreciate the relativity of human perception; this is why he rejects claims that the human intellect can fully grasp divine truth. Our lives are too full of change to allow us a consistent perspective. Yet, it is with the knowledge of these inadequacies that we are allowed an insight into the realities of existence; the force which Montaigne terms 'Nature' enables this insight. Consequently, we must brush aside the lure of theory and sharpen our sensitivities to our empirical understanding of life. Montaigne has a total confidence in the benevolence of the giver of life:

> J'accepte de bon coeur et recognoissant ce que nature a faict pour moy, et m'en agree et m'en loue. On fait tort à ce grand et tout puissant donneur de refuser son don, l'annuller et desfigurer. Tout bon, il a fait tout bon.

> I accept with a warm and grateful heart what nature has given me, and I delight in it and congratulate myself on it. It is to do wrong towards the great and all powerful giver to refuse his gift, to erase it and disfigure it. All good, he has made all good.
>
> (Montaigne 1962 III.XIII.1,094)

It is true that Montaigne stayed a Roman Catholic all his life and never openly criticized the Church. However, the times in which he lived were not conducive to open discussion about religion. His reasons for refusing to contest the authority of the Church may well have been the same as his reasons for avoiding political confrontation: his scepticism about the claims to authority of established power was equalled by a scepticism towards any other claimant to it. He was careful not to make pronouncements which assumed premises of which his experience could not inform him. This very reticence gave a greater strength to the assertions he did choose to make.

Winstanley also had considerable humility, which set him apart from some of the other radicals of his age. He did not, like the ranter Clarkson (Hill 1975: 215), consider himself justified by personal inclination alone. He humbled himself before laws created by a force beyond him, but in which he shared. Both Winstanley and Montaigne had an idea of being a part of an ultimately coherent creation which made sense of them. From the perception allowed them, they were able to evolve a confident critique of the unfairness and pretentiousness of their times. They were able to draw from their perception a peace of mind which survived independently of the unstable society around them. Neither saw militant confrontation as the right road to follow in their objection to injustice: to Winstanley violence was 'an abominable and unrighteous power'; to Montaigne war was

> la science de nous entredeffaire et entretuer, de ruiner et perdre nostre propre espece

> the knowledge of how to undo one another and to kill one another, to ruin and to destroy our own species
>
> > (Montaigne 1962: II.XII.452)

It might be said that the greed and gratuitous aggression which the civil wars in France, and then in England, had displayed led Montaigne and Winstanley to develop a contemplative and interior judgement which was able to see through the pretentiousness of civil authorities and to recognize the truth of human inadequacy. Calvin had achieved something similar. However, Calvin looked to grace alone to remedy these deficiencies. Montaigne and Winstanley found grace in their very experience, and felt they had found how life should rightly be lived.

Chapter 6

In the shadow of God: Andrew Marvell

The emphasis on action which flourished during the English Revolution encouraged those who witnessed it largely to immure themselves against the negative aspects of Calvin's original teaching. Preachers in England endeavoured to cultivate a sense of purpose, rather than to allow despair in personal resources of the kind that might well follow from a close exposure to Calvin's insistence on man's total inadequacy. Cromwell had no doubt that man should be 'up and doing', when what needed to be done was clear. When God had indicated what he wished man to do there was no question that self-interest would intervene. Winstanley extended this confidence in God's action to confidence in his own action: to him, his motives in digging the earth on George Hill were redolent with the values that constituted the essence of man's spiritual needs. However, both Cromwell and Winstanley were conscious of the need for a humility before the will of God, and acknowledged that they did not know themselves what course it might take. This humility was a legacy of Calvin's mistrust of humanity. It was a sobering feature of the thought of the Reform movement, and left its mark on many.

Calvin had urged his followers to recognize the worthlessness of human life, except inasmuch as it offers an experience of man's need of God. The writing of Andrew Marvell suggests the implicit presence of this attitude. Indeed, the tensions, paradoxes and challenges which constitute the fabric of his poetry echo the quandary of the human condition as Calvin described it. A fundamental difference is that Calvin presented this ravaged state of mind in a doctrinal manner; he analysed it clinically and objectively, presenting his conclusions as a self-evident truth. Marvell, however, demonstrates in his poetry the *experience* of being imprisoned in this contradictory condition. He shows how man's inclinations and pleasures prove insubstantial and misleading. The degree to which his poetry expresses delight in nature and in love has led to the impression that he is exclusively a lyric poet, envisaging an ideal harmony between man and his natural context. Much work has been done to establish Marvell in terms of the genres and conventions he adopted; the themes of his poems are often seen as mere counters in the game of prosody. However, if these themes are understood in terms of Calvin's suspicion of human inclination, and of the illusion of pleasure, a consistency emerges which suggests that Marvell's poems were conceived with such a perspective very much in mind.

It is clear that Andrew Marvell was exposed to a Calvinist way of thinking from an early age; indeed, his father was a lecturer at Holy Trinity Church, Hull, in the 1620s. He was amongst those preachers who were fundamental to the success of Puritan aims, and who reinforced the moral backbone of the Parliamentarians. indeed, resistance appeared to run in the Marvell family: the poet's grandfather moved away from Cambridge rather than pay a £2 fine levied by Charles I.

His father, also Andrew, was educated at a lately founded Puritan college, Emmanuel College, Cambridge, and was anxious that his son should equally receive a good education. He was sent firstly to Hull Grammar School, and subsequently to Trinity College, Cambridge, where he matriculated in 1633. This was a college devoted to erudition rather than to controversy. Several factors in his environment would appear to have led him away from Puritan criteria. He is reputed to have been lured by Jesuits to London in 1639, to be found by his father in a bookshop and subsequently returned to his studies in Cambridge (Legouis 1968: 4).

Whatever his personal opinions and experiences of these early days, it is certain that he acquired a wide knowledge. On the one hand he was taught scholastic exercises, a legacy from the Middle Ages, which he was later to mock. These mere rhetorical defences and assertions for the sake of the exercise alone had come into disrepute since Erasmus's early challenge of scholasticism. Marvell was not to mock all he learned at Cambridge, however. He benefited greatly from the interest in the study of languages which flourished at this time, which he was later to pursue more intensely in travel abroad. He was ultimately fluent in French, Italian and Spanish. He composed verse whilst at Cambridge, contributing to a volume assembled by the university in 1636 to celebrate the birth of Princess Anne, the queen's fifth child. This contribution was composed in both Greek and Latin.

In April 1640, Marvell's father drowned. Marvell left Cambridge shortly after, without completing his MA. He then went abroad for several years and there is no evidence of his return to England before 1648. He travelled widely, spending time in Holland, Italy, France and Spain.

There is little point in looking at the sparse indications of how Marvell spent his youth merely for anecdotal purposes. However, consideration of his early days suggests that his father played a seminal role in his life. A mind as responsive and as creative as that of Marvell must have been very conscious of the views of his outspoken father. Marvell's enemies were eventually to use memories of his father as a 'rebel and a schismatic' to taunt Marvell. Marvell acknowledged that his father was 'none of the most over running or eager' (Legouis 1968: 8) in the established rites of the Church of England; indeed, in 1639, a year before his death, he was reprimanded by the Archbishop for making insufficient use of the Book of Common Prayer in his sermons. He held conferences with Anabaptist and other sectaries. Unfortunately, none of the elder Marvell's sermons survive. However, there is no doubt as to the trend of his thinking, and of his mistrust of the established order.

When Andrew Marvell returned to England in 1648, he apparently mixed with Royalists. He had of course missed the major years of the fighting, although it cannot be said that he went abroad specifically to avoid them. He wrote poems that would appear to reflect sympathy for the Royalist cause, although with what degree of personal commitment it is impossible to assess. His poem to his noble friend Richard Lovelace, according to Legouis, expresses a 'Cavalier scorn for the vulgar herd' (Legouis 1968: 8). However, even at this early stage of his life, Marvell might well have already developed a sense of irony about passionate extremes; he recorded later that he was always inclined to favour the weaker party (Legouis 1968: 4).

Around 1650, a radical force took hold of his thinking which appears to have characterized it permanently. It was at this time that he wrote *An Horation Ode upon Cromwell's Return from Ireland*. This poem expresses a highly independent stance. No longer is Marvell writing to entertain friends, or to follow a particular fashion. He made no attempt to publish this work, which suggests that it was assembled so that he could himself think through the challenge that Cromwell presented. The *Ode upon Cromwell's Return* reflects several tensions and conflicts which operated in Marvell's mind. The poem begins with an acknowledgement of the need to see beyond the diversion of poetry and, instead of reading, to act:

'Tis time to leave the books in dust,
and oil th'unused armour's rust:

(Marvell 1986: 57, 5–6)

Immediately Marvell establishes an analogy with Cromwell, who, he says, transcended: 'the inglorious arts of peace' (ibid., 10), and followed the course of action God had set before him. Marvell links this concept with the idea of fate. Cromwell, he says, knowingly allied himself with this fate; he 'urged his active star' (ibid., 11) through going to war. Especially Marvell praises him for breaking his way 'through his own side' (ibid., 15), conscious that from the beginning of his involvement with the Parliamentarian army, Cromwell had to exert himself to transcend differences and to command the various factions within the anti-Royalists.

The overwhelming image of Cromwell that emerges is of a being controlled by a power beyond his own resources, to which he acquiesces. This acquiescence is shown as a form of wisdom:

Tis madness to resist or blame
The force of angry heaven's flame

(Marvell 1986: 57, 27–8)

Cromwell is presented as a man who forsook the retreat of his 'private gardens' where he had lived 'reserved and austere'. Driven by a force which defied pleasure and self-interest, he served to change totally the moral fabric of England:

and by industrious valour climb
To ruin the great work of time
And cast the kingdoms old
Into another mould

(Marvell 1986: 57, 33–6)

Already it is obvious that the points of tension in the poem are the insubstantial achievements of man, and the force of God's will, which drives beyond them. Cromwell is impelled by this force; what humanity has created (the kingdoms old, the great work of time) is destroyed. Notably 'Justice', another ancient concept, complains against Fate, pleading

the ancient rights in vain
(Marvell 1986: 57, 39)

At the beginning of the poem the need to be involved in armed conflict had diverted the young poet from cultural pursuits; similarly Cromwell had forsaken his rural retreat to embrace his destiny. All that had appeared civilized and sanctified by ancient tradition is now challenged and overthrown by a force beyond the control of man and understood only by someone, like Cromwell, in its command. The poem moves on to describe the execution of Charles I: he is shown as the epitome of elegance and restraint as he

bowed his comely head
down as upon a bed.
(Marvell 1986: 58, 63–4)

The loss of Charles's head is compared to the Roman discovery of a human head when the foundations of Rome were dug: England's 'happy fate' is said to be similarly augured.

The terms of Cromwell's triumph are clearly established in opposition to previously revered values. Marvell goes on to praise his humility:

How fit he is to sway
That can so well obey
(Marvell 1986: 58, 83–4)

Marvell shows Cromwell willingly subservient to forces beyond him, and ready to offer the fruits of his conquest to the nation.

And has his sword and spoils ungirt
To lay them at the public's skirt.
(Marvell 1986: 58, 89–90)

The poet foresees the liberation of 'all states not free' as the result of the force behind Cromwell's victories, and urges Cromwell to 'keep his sword erect' to maintain the power he has established. Marvell is not necessarily rejecting previous civilized values, but is certainly questioning the human ability to sustain them. The 'ancient rights', which include justice, only have value when men have the appropriate qualities:

those do hold or break
As men are strong or weak

(Marvell 1986: 58, 40–1)

Cromwell is shown as a man 'that does both act and know'. His willingness to act, acknowledging a force beyond him, demonstrates a superiority to the weaknesses of men of the 'kingdom old'.

Critics have commented on the affection and respect for the late king which Marvell suggests in his portrayal of Charles I's death. This nostalgia for courtly values, contrasted with a fierce assertion of the inevitability of the power of another force, constitutes the duality which sustains much of Marvell's poetry. This duality is consistent with Calvinist ideology. It has been described by Christopher Hill as a conflict between subjective and objective, between 'ideals and the brute reality of the civil war' (Hill 1957: 342). Elsewhere, Christopher Hill refers to this 'brute reality' as 'fate' or the 'Historic process'. Rephrasing this idea in Calvinist terms, the inscrutable forces are identifiable as the will of God, acting in terms which defy immediate comprehension but which, fundamentally, have a far greater significance than the mere achievements of man. Marvell associates Cromwell with this force, not because of any intrinsic merit of his own, but because he is willing to acquiesce before it.

Marvell's poetry from the early 1650s onwards derives its impact from the tensions between human experience and the terms imposed upon it from beyond humanity. Marvell depicts vivid human response, together with an acknowledgement of a power beyond it, which undermines its intrinsic coherence.

A Dialogue Between the Soul and Body expresses man's inability to resolve the problems presented by the conflict between spiritual and physical within him. The theme of the poem is reminiscent of St Paul's epistle to the Galatians (5: 17) 'For the flesh lusteth against the spirit, and the spirit against the flesh: and these are contrary one to the other: so that ye cannot do the things ye would.' The account of the soul's predicament in Marvell's poem suggests that man's spiritual yearnings are compromised by the restrictions of the body. Paradoxically, the very abilities which the physicality of man is meant to ensure – seeing, hearing – are obstructed spiritually by their limitations, confined as they are to the material world. The soul complains of being

Here blinded with an eye: and there
Deaf with the drumming of an ear.

(Marvell 1986: 17, 5–6)

This idea is reminiscent of Gloucester's speech in *King Lear*:

I stumbled when I saw: full oft 'tis seen
Our means secure us . . .

(*King Lear*, IV. i. 20–1)

Conversely, in Marvell's poem, the body is shown to be unable to relax in its physicality alone: the human condition is such that man is constantly beset by some spiritual anxiety. As Calvin said, the mark which God implanted within us serves as a continual reminder of our inadequacy and inherent sinfulness. The description of the human being at the mercy of sickness, the 'pestilence of love', as well as the palsy, shows the greatest torment as caused by 'sorrow's other madness'. This state of defeat is imposed by 'knowledge': an apprehension of the will of God which will allow no reconciliation with mere physical appetite. Finally the soul is shown as an 'architect', hewing the green trees which once grew wild in the forest. Man's nature, which yearns for solace through satisfying the demands of his physical existence, is coerced by his apprehension of the laws of God into another form.

The opposition between the spiritual and the lure of the pleasure of material existence is nowhere clearer than in Marvell's *Dialogue Between the Resolved Soul and Created Pleasure*. Pleasure describes her delights with vivid imagery of fruits, flowers and physical comfort; later in the poem more sophisticated pleasures – music, money, love, power and knowledge – are held out to lure the soul, but the soul is resolute and prefers the values of conscience and humility to the delights proferred by created pleasure. The terms of this poem are perhaps less challenging than some of Marvell's others, since the structure is apparently so uncompromising. However, it is notable that the lyricism of pleasure's account of herself is aesthetically engaging to the reader, and the soul's tart rejoinder less so. The soul's rejection of music is none the less reluctant, and her admission to its loveliness is endearing in its vulnerability:

Soul: Had I but any time to lose
On this I would it all dispose

(Marvell 1986: 23, 41–2)

The soul declares that music above all is close to reconciling her to the human condition. But still she resists; once freed from this, there is no further risk:

> None can chain a mind
> Whom this sweet chordage cannot bind
> (Marvell 1986: 23, 43–4)

This poem suggests that the *poetic* dimension of Marvell's mind, the faculty which recreates and rephrases in imagery different aspects of the experience of pleasure, is intrinsically bound with its fundamental humanity (as is the soul's love of music). The intellectual, morally committed element is ready to build in arid axioms to confine or to reject the rest. At the end of this poem, the soul dedicates herself to humility: to submission to a force beyond human resources, which places these in appropriate proportion.

Marvell's love poetry is valued for its vivid intensity, adding an apparently defeatist irony to the paradoxes of other metaphysical love poetry. However, this poetry expresses more than a personal state of mind. It is possible to see Marvell's depiction of the power of love as exemplary of the quandary of the human condition, as understood in the tradition of negative theology. Marvell shows his reader a mind enslaved by a power it cannot resist, incapable of drawing on any resources capable of delivering it. Humanity is shown in all its vulnerability to a power which destroys it, and yet with which it colludes.

The mower in *The Mower's Song* fondly remembers his affection for the meadows, over which he had control:

> When Juliana came, and she
> What I do to the grass, doth to my thoughts and me
> (Marvell 1986: 36, 11–12)

Love is presented as a source of disintegration of integrity. Marvell's poem *The Definition of Love* brings in many of the terms used in the *Ode on Cromwell's Return*: similarly, tension is shown between human illusions and the uncompromising force of an ultimate reality:

> And yet I quickly might arrive
> Where my extended soul is fixed,
> But Fate does iron weges drive,
> And crowds itself betwixt
>
> (Marvell 1986: 25, 11–14)

Fate, the 'opposition of the stars', establishes decrees of steel which demand and destroy the sense of justification of human emotion. Marvell's poetry expresses the plight of the defeated lover from the lover's viewpoint, but that does not mean that he is exonerating this legendary folly. *The Unfortunate Lover* again shows the lover as a victim of fate – in other words, of his human condition. He is portrayed as helpless, reared by cormorants, fed with

> hopes and air,
> Which soon digested to despair.
>
> (Marvell 1986: 43, 33–4)

He is called on to duel with fortune at the command of an angry heaven, wishing to behold a spectacle of blood. The final image is that of a plagued and defenceless wretch, his only dignity lying in his futile efforts to reject his plight:

> See how he nak'd and fierce does stand,
> Cuffing the thunder with one hand
>
> (Marvell 1986: 43, 49–50)

The image is reminiscent of a chained dancing bear. Marvell presents a victim rather than a prisoner: the impact of the poem lies in its inference that reader and writer are as vulnerable as the victim. All are victimized by the human condition. The poem ends accusing the 'malignant stars', the fate which has augured things, so that Love is

> Forced to live in storms and wars
> Yet dying leaves a perfume here,
> And music within every ear.
>
> (Marvell 1986: 44, 60–3)

In the contrast between stark inevitability and the pathos of human suffering, there are similarities here to Marvell's description of Charles I's death in *Ode to Cromwell's Return*.

Although Marvell scoffs at human pretentiousness, he is ready to admire realism in the face of a loaded situation. This emerges in

To his Coy Mistress. In this poem, Marvell deflates the pose of a woman defying seduction. He states acerbically that her reluctance means only that she is willing herself to death, since nothing else awaits her. There is no victory, the poem declares, in maintaining this meaningless pose. The invitation to

> tear our pleasures with rough strife
> Through the iron gates of life
>
> (Marvell 1986: 42, 43–4)

demolishes through its forceful physicality all euphemism. The 'deserts of vast eternity' which the poet calls upon his mistress to envisage lying before them is very much like Pascal's 'silence eternel de ces espaces infinies'; such vastness reduces human pretention, even human emotion, to nothing.

In Marvell's poetry, love appears as a force to which man is helplessly susceptible: as in the plays of Racine, it is a revealing affliction, showing the essential weakness of the human will and the inherent capacity of the human condition for self-destruction. Reared as a Jansenist, Racine was familiar with the Augustinian theology which states that to follow the self was to follow sin, and that, without grace, man could not prevent this. Both Racine and Marvell portray the interiority of this experience.

Marvell is well known as 'the poet of gardens', and again, obvious references to his personal experience give his poetry on this theme much of its impact. The garden is an ambiguous image, with at least the two obvious references to the garden of Eden and the Garden of Gethsemane expanding on the personal experience of a place of refreshment. In the seventeenth century, the garden was for many a bourgeois luxury. Marvell's poem *The Garden* describes an idyllic tranquillity to be found there, but the soul, he adds, is prepared for 'longer flight' (Marvell 1986: 49, 55). In *Upon Appleton House*, Marvell describes the gardens at the house of his employer, Lord Fairfax, the former general of the Parliamentarian army. He vividly depicts the harvest, and describes himself as 'languishing with ease' in this beautiful place, rich in trees, vines and flowers. But then, at the climax of the poem, he is alerted to the presence of young Maria, Fairfax's daughter, whom he has been employed to tutor. Marvell then embarks on a panegyric of Maria's moral virtues, which far outshine the beauty nature has to offer:

Tis she that to these gardens gave
That wondrous beauty which they have;

                         (Marvell 1986: 19, 689–90)

There is indeed poetic conceit in the comparison between Maria's 'straightness' and 'sweetness' with that of the woods and meadows, but her moral qualities are the most strongly stressed. Mary Fairfax is praised for her modesty; she does not even wish to see her beauty reflected in the brook. The savage tones of *To his Coy Mistress* are echoed here, as Marvell berates vain women, unlike Mary:

        your own face shall at you grin,
Thorough the black bag of your skin

                         (Marvell 1986: 19, 733–4)

Fairfax, too, is the object of eulogy in this poem:

For he did, with his utmost skill,
Ambition weed but conscience till

                         (Marvell 1986: 78, 353–4)

There is no doubt that Marvell admired certain human qualities. Predominantly, however, these relate to self-effacement. He admired Cromwell for his readiness to submit to 'the force of angry heaven's flame'. Cromwell's action in carrying forward the Revolution and framing the Commonwealth raised him above the ranks of common man, who

        declining alwayes, disappears
In the weak circle of increasing years

                         (Marvell 1986: 94, 3–4)

Marvell was as certain as other Puritans of his time that the events which had overtaken England in the mid-seventeenth century indeed manifested the will of God. It is in terms of his response to this that Marvell portrays Cromwell. Just as Cromwell himself insisted on his personal subservience to God's will, so Marvell insisted on the essential futility of the life of man without grace:

        his short tumults of themselves dispose,
While flowing Time above his head doth close

                         (Marvell 1986: 94, 5–6)

Marvell's praise of Cromwell is best read as a hymn to the power of God. He makes a point, in his commemoration of Cromwell's first anniversary in power, of Cromwell's being 'alone' in this visitation of grace to command him. In comparison, others dwindle.

Basically, Marvell's suspicion of mere human adequacy is the force behind his irony. In a way similar to the technique adopted by Pascal, Marvell diminishes man's sense of self-importance. Just as Pascal, in the *Pensées*, shows all man's points of reference to be insubstantial, and his sense of proportion to be invalid, so Marvell presents man in a perspective that reduces him entirely. A passage from *Upon Appleton House* illustrates this:

> And now to the Abyss I pass
> Of that unfathomable grass,
> Where men like grasshoppers appear,
> But grasshoppers like giants there:
> They in their squeaking laugh condemn
> Us as we walk more low than them
>
> (Marvell 1986: 78, 369–74)

Again, but in a different genre, Marvell emphasizes the disparity between man's sense of self-importance and another perspective, in his letter to Sir John Trott in June 1664 on the death of his son. Marvell points out the disproportion between the concern of an individual and the dimension of God's will:

> Though in respect of an only gourd an only Son be inestimable, Yet, in comparison to God, man bears a thousand times less proportion: so that it is like Jonah's sin to be angry with God for the withering of his Shadow.
>
> (Marvell 1952: 71)

Marvell's parliamentary career as member for Hull implies his impatience with pretentiousness. His own fulfilment of his commitment to his constituents was exemplary: he sent detailed and accurate reports to them on a regular basis of all proceedings in parliament. As member of the opposition party to Charles II, he maintained the case for democracy and religious freedom, commitments which he had shared with Milton. His sense of irony and readiness to ridicule the self-importance of men in power none the less still found expression. In his mock speech from the throne of Charles II, he ridicules the ready aquiescence of the king to any favours parliament might be prepared to bestow on him (Marvell

1986: 160). Similarly, in *The Rehearsal Transpos'd*, he challenges the Anglican Samuel Parker on the integrity of his faith, exposing his behaviour as based on conceit, very much as Molière exposes Tartuffe, his fraudulent bigot. In *The Rehearsal Transpos'd*, Marvell blames Archbishop Laud for the degeneration of the Anglican Church into 'Arminian subtleties' (Marvell 1986: 149): the Church had become a means for gentlemen to recover that 'ancient glory' and to restore pomp and ceremony. All this 'laziness and splendour' was obstructed by Puritans, and the gentry were keen to exact revenge.

These terms, although part of a totally different genre, are reminiscent of the 'ancient world', described in *The Ode on Cromwell's Return*, which had reached a point of decadence ready for Cromwell's demolition. The way in which Marvell proceeds to describe the onset of the civil wars in *The Rehearsal Transpos'd* is penetrating and memorable:

> Whether it were a war of religion, or of liberty, is not worth the labour to enquire. Whichsoever was at the top, the other was at the bottom; but considering all, I think the Cause was too good to have been fought for.

> (Marvell 1986: 150)

This statement is not cynical; on the contrary, it brings home the difference Marvell perceived between the 'grasshopper' status of man, and the directive of 'heaven's flame'. This distinction gave Marvell a stability in his satiric stance, so that his satire, as well as his lyric poetry, deflates the delusions men create.

Chapter 7

Conclusion

I hope that my discussion of the writings considered in the previous chapters will have offered interesting samples from a spectrum of views on man's relation with God at a time of social upheaval. It is clear that the concept man has of God affects the concept he has of himself and of the validity of his action. In this way, it is possible to observe the differences in identity which each of the aforementioned writers conferred on himself. It is with a consideration of this that I shall conclude.

Calvin's presentation is essentially didactic. He writes to teach, and therefore to him the justice of the content of his lesson validates his identity. Through his knowledge of the Bible Calvin thought to have ascertained absolute truths about the total inadequacy of the human condition, and man's total dependence on the grace of God. It was his vocation to communicate these truths, and to do his best to enlighten other men. His reading of St Augustine led him to insist on a radical division between the 'city of man' and the 'city of God'. Enslaved by sin, men were inevitably drawn to the former, and would pursue their self-interest alone. Calvin hoped to remind his readers of the delusion of this behaviour. His recommendation was that men should humble themselves in prayer and set no store by their own competence.

Man's involvement in society reflected the need for these priorities, in Calvin's eyes. He thought that nothing of God's ordinance could be established by man, and that therefore it was folly to endeavour to undermine any existing social order in the hope of substituting a more equitable one. To Calvin, the justice of man and the justice of God were infinitely at odds. This rift is expressed succinctly in his commentary on St Paul's Epistle to the Romans, X. 2:

Premierement, nous voyons que ces deux manieres de justice sont opposees l'une a l'autre comme choses contraires, et qui ne peuvent subsister ensemble. Dont s'ensuit que la justice de Dieu est mise bas et renversee, si tost que les hommes establissent la leur propre

Above all, we see that these two kinds of justice are opposed one to the other like contrary things, and which may not exist together. Whereby it follows that the justice of God is brought down and toppled as soon as men establish their own [justice]

This absolute disparity would have made nonsense of any direct commitment to militant action, if the intention were to establish a social order more worthy than the one it sought to destroy. The need to defend the survival of freedom of worship alone led Calvin to sympathize with those who took up arms to do so. He made it clear that the criteria of self-protection and of personal superiority were entirely inappropriate for defenders of the faith to adopt. If anything, their trials should serve to remind them of their total dependence on God, and they should not read into the circumstances of their military position any signs of God's favour.

In his commentaries and writing, Calvin adopts the first person plural to establish his stance. This pedagogic technique absorbs the reader's response to his text. It guards against an implication of instrinsic superiority, and suggests that Calvin too is involved directly in spiritual challenges that God presents to humanity.

The work of d'Aubigné follows, theologically, the same premises as Calvin: man is enmeshed in a morass of sin from which only grace can deliver him. But rather than dismiss in general terms the destructive demands of society, as Calvin, from his pulpit, is free to do, d'Aubigné undertakes the arduous task of examining his own immediate situation, unremittingly involved as he was in the plight of the persecuted Reformers. D'Aubigné's experience of the misery of his country and his own inner distress provide material for a portrayal of the afflictions of sin, but the corollary, the pole of truth which lies in God, is beyond the terms of a human poetic account. It is supplied in d'Aubigné's psalm meditation, and his epic poem, *Les Tragiques*, by quotation and paraphrase drawn from the Bible, with remarkably little intervention on the part of the writer to adapt it to the specific demands of his own text. In the psalm meditations, the Bible acts as a point of reference that gives human experience its proper proportion. The continued inclusion of what he considers to be passages from the Scriptures in *Les Tragiques* establishes the true perspective of his account of the confusion of his times. D'Aubigné tells his readers how he has strained to follow the illumination offered by the prophets of the Old Testament:

> La ou estoyent les feux des prophetes plus vieux
> Je tends comme je puis le cordeau de mes yeux
>
> There, where shine the beacons of the oldest prophets,
> I strain as I might the strength of my eyes
>
> (L.T.: 1, 37)

When he introduces images or concepts drawn directly from Biblical texts, he is anxious to point out the differences between these and mere human device. The reader might expect some indulgent imaginative fantasy:

> Ici le vain lecteur desja en l'air s'esgare
> L'esprit mal prepare fantastic se prepare
> A voir quelques discours de monstres inventés
>
> Here the vain reader is already lost in mid-air
> The ill-prepared spirit in his own fantasy prepares
> To see some exposition of invented monsters
>
> (L.T.: 6, 73)

However, the visions which will appear in d'Aubigné's poem will not be his inventions:

> Ainsi les visions qui seront ici peintes
> Seront exemples vrais de nos histoires saintes
>
> So, the visions which will be painted here
> Will be true examples of our holy Scriptures
>
> (L.T.: 6, 89)

This distinction between the vain imaginings of man, and the substantial, which is the will of God, recurs throughout the poem.

The task of adjusting the focus of Biblical insight to obtain a full understanding of his time, and of his own sin, was an aim d'Aubigné set himself, and felt, ultimately, inadequate to effect.

An overwhelming sense of the negligible resources of humanity, including his own poetic gifts, pervades d'Aubigné's work. Only when purged of sin would he be free from his inadequacies. This will only be achieved beyond the present life. The identity which d'Aubigné confers on himself in his work is ridden with impotence. He prays God to take this identity away from him: 'separe moy de moy'.

D'Aubigné's rejection of the resources of the human condition contrasts strongly with the self-confidence assumed by some of his fellow Reformers in the 1570s. The identity projected by the Monomachs is one of united invincibility, at least on a moral front. The sense of being God's chosen increased, and presenting themselves as the tribe of Israel proved a source of solidarity. Calvin was suspicious of any tendency to read God's will in immediate events, although he insisted that history showed God's will at work. In terms of man's present life, however, to Calvin God was unknowable. Increasingly, Reformers saw themselves as the representatives of God's justice. Whereas Calvin had stressed that there could be no fusion between God's justice and that of man, the Monomachs established a vivid contrast between their values and those of their enemies: they were diametrically opposed. What to their opponents was truth was to the Reformers falsehood.

This new-found confidence in the surety of human judgement was a watershed in the religious and political thinking of the Reform. It established itself amongst the English Calvinists. John Foxe in his widely read *English Book of Martyrs* 'conditioned generations of English Protestants to a belief in the historic mission of their role' (Lamont 1969: 23). The conviction of their importance in the mind of God led to a sense of being able to read the mind of God. In this way of thinking, the judgement of God and the judgement of man were close enough to justify action.

In the conditions which led to the English Revolution, confidence in judgement was essential. Cromwell was able to develop this, largely, thanks to his tutor, Thomas Beard, who had shown that God's presence in history was no less apparent than his presence in everyday occurence.

Oliver Cromwell was able to build a state of mind which trusted essentially in God, but which had confidence in the human ability to read God's judgements, so that he felt he was able to co-operate with it. The Parliamentary cause was insolubly linked in Cromwell's mind with God's will, and his allegiance to it enabled him to go into battle with the confidence of God's approval. His many accounts of victories which had no objective reason to explain them demonstrate how a whole dimension of his strategy depended on faith. His build-up of clauses describing action, which ends with the single statement 'and God did it', provides a vivid example of how he understood the evolution of events. Cromwell's insistence on the disparity between his own identity and the workings of God's will cannot be too much emphasized. He retained throughout his life a humility which left his mind open, and took decisive action only when compelled to do so.

His principal aim was to be tolerant, not repressive, since his humility reminded him that there were more things in heaven and earth than he could necessarily account for.

The contrast with Winstanley's outlook is illuminating. It might at first be deduced that Winstanley's confidence in human judgement was, if anything, greater than that of the wary Cromwell. But Cromwell's readiness to read immediate religious significance into the events of his time was far more specific than Winstanley's. For Winstanley, Cromwell's frame of reference was too parochial. Winstanley objected strongly to any aspect of the social structure, as it then was, being identified with the will of the creator. His confidence in the human judgement he observed amongst his fellow men was negligible. Man had clouded his judgement, in Winstanley's eyes; he had allowed himself to be seduced by the lure of property, and by delusions of others' spurious authority. He was responsible for his own corruption. There is therefore a vast polarity in Winstanley's view of things. On the one hand, he was unreservedly critical of the way in which men had established society. On the other, he believed that the insight afforded to him, and therefore available to others, offered the means to overturn these injustices, and to rebuild society on the principles of working together and common ownership. The concept Winstanley had of his creator allowed him immeasurable inner freedom. Because of this, the identity he conferred upon himself was essentially interior; it had no feasible role in the society of his time. His action in digging on George Hill was, inevitably, merely symbolic. There was no integration between what was viable and what, to him, was absolute. As a result, the Digger colonies were obliterated. In no time, Winstanley was forgotten and may even have forgotten himself the dream that his sense of the needs of humanity led him to conceive.

Marvell in many ways epitomizes the separation between man and God which Calvin had defined. His helpless discomfort is not intended as a display of his awareness of a religious dimension in his life, and is all the more powerful for that. His mind had absorbed the irony of negative theology, so that any activity to which he found himself drawn was inevitably self-destructive. Although it is clear that he was a responsible member of parliament for Hull, the force of his presence lay in his ability to see through pretentious pose. And yet, his early verse on Cromwell suggests that he believed in the possibility of a force beyond man which had the power to put right what man had ruined. In Marvell's mind, this force could in no way be allied with human action through human will.

References

Allen, J.W. (1957) *A History of Political Thought in the 16th Century*, London.

Abbott, W.C. (ed.) (1937–47) *The Writings and Speeches of Oliver Cromwell*, Cambridge, Mass.: 4 vols.

Aubigné, Agrippa d' (1886–1909) *Histoire Universelle*, Paris, ed. A. de Ruble: 10 vols.

—— (1945) *Pages Inédités* Geneva, ed. P.P. Plan.

—— (1948) *Le Printemps L'hecatombe a Diane*, Geneva, ed. P. Gegnebin.

—— (1962–7) *Les Tragiques*, Paris, ed. A. Garnier and J. Plattard.

—— (1967) *Oeuvres Complètes*, Geneva, ed. E. Reaume and J. de Caussade: 3 vols.

Augustine, Saint (1924) *De Civitate Dei*, London, ed. J. Welldon.

Barnaud, Nicolas (1573) *Dialogue auquel sont traitées plusieurs choses advenues aux Lutheriens et Huguenots de la France*, Basel.

Beard, Thomas (1631) *The Theatre of God's Judgements*, London.

Bèze, Théodore de (1560) *Traicté de l'Authorité des Magistrats en la Punition des Heretiques, & du moyen d'y proceder*, Geneva.

—— (1964) *Chrestiennes Méditations*, Geneva, ed. Richter.

—— (1960–83) *Correspondance*, Geneva, ed. A. Dufour: 11 vols.

Calvin, Jean (1546) *Deux Sermons faitz en la ville de Geneve l'un le mercredy 4eme de novembre 1545 apres avoir ouy nouelles que les papistes avoyent esmeu guerre en Allemagne contre les Chrestiens. Le second, le mercredy prochainement suyvant, apres que nouelles furent venues que Dieu avoit donne victoire aux siens*, etc., Geneva.

—— (1552a) *Commentaire sur le Prophete Isaie*, Geneva.

—— (1552b) *Preface de Jehan Calvin touchant l'utilité des Pseaumes et de la translation presente*, in *Les Pseaumes de David, traduicts selon la verite Hebraique avec annotations tresutiles par Loys Budé*, Geneva.

—— (1552–4) *Le Premier Livre des Commentaires de M. Iean Calvin sur les Actes des Apostres*, Geneva.

—— (1563a) *Commentaires sur le livre des Pseaumes*, Geneva.

—— (1563b) *Sermons de M. Iean Calvin sur le Livre de Iob*, Geneva.

—— (1565a) *Quarante Sept Sermons de M. Iean Calvin sur les huict derniers chapitres des Propheties de Daniel*, La Rochelle.

—— (1565b) *Lecons ou Commentaires et expositions de Iean Calvin tant sur les Revelations que sur les lamentations du prophete Ieremie*, Lyon.

—— (1567) *Sermons de M. Iean Calvin sur le Verme livre de Moyse nomme Dueteronome*, Geneva.

—— (1854) *Lettres*, Paris, ed. J. Bonnet: 2 vols.

—— (1863–1900) *Opera qui supersunt omnia*, Brunswick, ed. G. Baum, E. Cunitz, F. Reuss and Erichson: Corpus Reformatorum, 59 vols.

—— (1954) *Commentaire de M. Iean Calvin sur le 1er livre de Moyse, dit Genese*, Geneva.

—— (1957–68) *Institution de la religion Chrestienne*, Paris, ed. J.D. Benoit: 5 vols.

—— (1970) *Three French Treatises*, London, ed. F. Higman.

Cave, Terence C. (1969) *Devotional Poetry in France, c. 1570–1613*, Cambridge.

Cohn, Norman (1957) *The Pursuit of the Millennium*, London.

Dickens, A.G. (1966) *Reformation and Society in 16th Century Europe*, London.

Du Bartas, G. de Saluste (1974) *La Judit*, Toulouse, ed. Baiche.

Geisendorf, P.F. (1949) *Theodore de Bèze*, Geneva.

Goulard, S. (1578) *Mémoires de l'Etat de France sous Charles I*, Heidelberg, ed. S. Goulard: 3 vols.

—— *Assavoir s'il est loisible aux suiets de se deffendre contre le Magistrat, pour maintenir la Religion vrayment Chrestienne*.

—— *Assavoir s'il est licite sauver la vie aux massacreurs et aux bourreaux prins en guerre par ceux de la Religion assiegez en ceste ville*.

Gregg, P. (1986) *Free Born John (A Biography of John Lilburne)*, London.

Hay, Denys (9177) *Annalists and Historians: Western Historiography from the 8th Century to the 18th Century*, London.

Hill, Christopher (1957) *Puritanism and Revolution*, London.

—— (1973) *God's Englishman*, London.

—— (1975) *The World Turned Upside Down*, London.

—— 1977) *Milton and the English Revolution*, London.

—— (1986) *Collected Essays*, Brighton.

—— (1990) *A Nation of Change and Novelty*, London.

Kelley, D.R. (1970) *The Foundation of Modern Historical Scholarship: Language, Law and History in the French Renaissance*, Columbia.

—— (1991) *The Beginning of Ideology: Consciousness and Society in the French Reformation*, Cambridge.

Kingdon, Robert M. (1956) *Geneva and the Coming of the Wars of Religion in France 1555–1563*, Geneva.

—— (1967) *Geneva and the Consolidation of the French Protestant Movement 1564–1572*, Geneva.

Lagarde, Georges de (1926) *Recherches sur l'Esprit Politique de la Réforme*, Paris.

Lamont, William (1969) *Godly Rule: Politics and Religion 1603–1660*, London.

Languet, Hubert (pseud?) or Brutus (1581) *De la Puissance Legitime du Prince sur le Peuple et du Peuple sur le Prince (Vindiciae contra Tyrannos)*, Geneva.

Lefebvre, L. (1971) *La Naissance de l'historiographie moderne*, Paris.

Legouis, Pierre (1968) *Andrew Marvell, Poet, Puritan, Patriot*, London.

L'Hôpital, Michel de (1822–6) *Oeuvres complètes,* Paris: 5 vols.

Marvell, Andrew (1952) *The Poems of Andrew Marvell,* London, ed. H. Macdonald.

—— (1986) *Andrew Marvell, Selected Poetry and Prose,* London, ed. R. Wilcher.

Mesnard, Pierre (1956) *L'Essor de la Philosophie Politique au XVIe Siecle,* Paris.

Milton, J. (1953) *De Doctrina Christiana,* Yale, ed. D.M. Wolfe.

Montaigne, Michel de (1962) *Oeuvres complètes,* Paris.

Morrill, John (1990) *Oliver Cromwell and the English Revolution,* London.

Pascal, B. (1960) *Pensées,* Paris, ed. L. Lafuma.

Phillips, Margaret Mann (1967) *Erasmus on his Times,* Cambridge.

Salmon, J. (1974) *The French Wars of Religion,* Boston, Mass.

Skinner, Quentin (1978) *The Foundations of Modern Political Thought,* Cambridge: 2 vols.

Soulié, Marguerite (1977) *L'Inspiration Biblique dans la poésie religieuse d'Agrippa d'Aubigné,* Paris.

Sutherland, N.M. (1967) *Calvin's Idealism and Indecision in the French Wars of Religion,* Boston, Mass.

Tawney, R.H. (1938) *Religion and the Rise of Capitalism,* London.

Wencelius, Leon (1937) *L'Esthétique de Calvin,* Paris.

Winstanley, Gerrard (1941) *The Works of Gerrard Winstanley,* New York, ed. G.H. Sabine.

—— (1973) *The Law of Freedom and Other Writings,* London.

Index

DATE DUE

			Printed in USA